Driving Tours
and
Short Walks

Edited by
Sam Moore

Sligo

*Highwood Community
Resource Centre Ltd
1999*

Highwood Community Resource Centre Ltd

PROJECT EDITOR   Sam Moore.

RESEARCHERS   Barry Briggs, Lilly Briggs, Kathleen Casey, Attracta Conlon,
                            Moira Doyle, Margaret Hegarty, Anne Kelly, Edmund Lawless,
                            Alisair Lawson, James Lynch, Patricia Mayo, Terrie McDonagh,
                            Sam Moore.

PROJECT CO-ORDINATORS   Sam Moore, Martina Walsh.

PHOTOGRAPHY   t = top, tl = top left, tr = top right, b = bottom, bl = bottom left
                            br = bottom right, c = centre

Sam Moore - cover inset, title page, 5b, 6tr, 6br, 8, 11tl, 12, 13, 15tr, 15b, 16tl, 18tl, 18c, 19tr, 20t, 20b, 23br, 25t, 25tl, 26tl, 26c, 26b, 29t, 29b, 30b, 31b, 32bl, 37tl, 38tr, 38b, 39tr, 40t, 45, 46bl, 50tl, 52bl, 52br, 54tl, 55t, 58, 59br, 62bl, 64, 65tl, 66tr, 72, 76br 77t, 77br, 78t, 78bl, 79b, 81t, 81b, 82tl, 82bl, 83tl, 84tl, 84b, 85br, 85t, 90br, 91tl, 91bl. **Alistair Lawson** - 6bl, 50br, 51, 57, 60t, 63tl, 65b. **Mary Rohan** - 7tl, 15t, 17c, 24br, 41tl, 47b, 53tl, 53c,53bl, 54br, 55br, 63b, 67, 75, 80bl, 83tr, 88bl, 89tl, 91c, 91br, 92tr. **Mike Bunn** cover, facing page 1, 21, 42, 43t, 49t, 56t, 56b. **Sean Duignan** - 10, 11br, 14 16br, 25br, 35br, 39b, 40br, 43bl, 47t, 49br, 59tl, 60, 68br, 69, 70, 71, 76t, 79t, 86b, 87t, 89b. **Ballintrillick Environmental Group** - 5tr, 33b, 43br. **Bob Shanley** - contents page, 61b, 62tl, 88c. **North West Tourism** - 1, 7br, 9, 19b, 28t, 28bl, 34, 35t, 36, 44tl, 44br, 48, 52, 66b, 70tr, 70bl, 74b, 80tl, 87br, 88t. **National Museum of Ireland** - 37tr, 41b, 46c, 74t. **Royal Irish Academy** - 68tl, 80c, 82c. **Anne and Michael Yeats** - 17. **Lough Gill Environmental Project** - 22tl, 22bl, 23t, 24t, 25c, 30tr, 30c, 31tl, 31br, 32t, 33t, 46br. **Slide File** - 26b, Michael Arden - 83bl, 90t.

MAPS   The maps in this book were a special commission for a private
                            collection and painted in oils by Mary Rohan. We are extremely
                            grateful to Christy and Moira Tighe for allowing us to use them.

Mary Rohan is a Sligo based artist. Her work is exhibited in Ireland and abroad. Specific to Sligo she has illustrated flora and fauna guides to Hazelwood and Doorly Park nature trails for Coillte and Sligo County Council. She also designed a stone engraving situated overlooking Lough Gara which depicts the area. She is also responsible for designing the symbols used for each of the tours in this book.

DESK TOP PUBLISHING   Sam Moore.

Published by **Highwood Community Resource Centre Ltd,** Highwood, Kilmactranny, County Sligo, Ireland. Tel.: 00 353 (0)78 47500, Email: highwood@tinet.ie

ISBN   0 9536065 0 3

Acknowledgements
This booklet was produced by Lough Arrow Research Project through a partnership approach involving Highwood Community Resource Centre Ltd, FÁS Community Services Unit, Sligo County Council, Sligo LEADER Partnership Company, Marketing Sligo Forum, North West Tourism, and Arrow Community Enterprises Ltd.

Particular thanks to John O'Neill, Christy Tighe, Anna Jones, Damien Brennan, Collette O'Brien, Des Clarke, John McHugh, Martina Walsh, Maurice Gannon, John Williams of Coillte, Mike Bunn, Ed and Lynn McGrath, Bob Shanley, Ballintrillick Environmental Group, Mary Rohan, Ann Yeats, John McTernan, Martin Byrne, Fiona and Isabel Moore, Michael Arden, Frank Kelly, the Royal Irish Academy, the National Museum of Ireland and Sligo County Library.

Every effort has been made to ensure that the information in this book is accurate. However, details such as phone numbers, opening hours, etc are liable to change. The publishers cannot accept responsibility for any consequences arising from the use of this book. The publisher in no way is liable or responsible for any injury or loss to any person using this book.

Contact Highwood Community Resource Centre at above address to order copies.

Contents

Introduction
Welcome to Sligo 1
Driving in County Sligo 5
A note on the short walks included in this guide ... 5
Sligo Naturally 7
William Butler Yeats 8

Sligo City Walking Tour
Sligeach - the Place of Shells 9

Mountain of the Two Birds Tour
a circuit of Lough Gill 21

Boar of Benbulben Tour
a tour of Yeats Country and North County Sligo ... 33

Queen Maeve Tour
a tour of the Coolera Peninsula, the eastern Ox
Mountains and the coast to Aughris Head 45

The Labby Tour
a drive around the Lough Arrow region 57

The Bardic Tour
a tour through the Ox Mountains and the
northern coastline of Tireragh Barony 69

The Corran Tour
a tour of Ballymote, Gurteen and Lough Gara
in south County Sligo 81

Benbulben

Welcome to Sligo

Sligo is a land of startling contrasts with a diversity of spectacular scenery and landscapes. From a coastline broken by bays and inlets and golden deserted beaches the wooded countryside rolls inland around placid lakes, to be stopped abruptly by sheer limestone ridges such as Benbulben. Further inland, after the glaciers of the last Ice Age receded around 10,000 years ago, one of Ireland's most beautiful and unspoilt areas was revealed, sculpted with valleys and shimmering with lakes.

One of the smaller counties of Ireland, Sligo contains everything a person could wish for; not just the huge range of natural charms and amenities, but also its superb traditional music and warmth of the people. Sligo has one of the richest concentrations of prehistoric and later monuments in Western Europe with over 5,000 recorded archaeological sites - from one of the world's oldest and largest megalithic cemeteries at Carrowmore to the ancient castles of Sligo's clans. The beauty of the countryside and its fascinating blend of myth, legend and history have inspired poets, artists and scholars throughout time. The most notable influence was on the works of Ireland's Nobel Prize winning poet, William Butler Yeats, who was greatly influenced by this magical land. He called Sligo 'the Land of Heart's Desire'. His brother, the artist Jack Yeats, used to say that he never painted a picture without thinking of Sligo.

The purpose of this booklet is to help you gain the most out of a visit to Sligo. It is made up of six driving tours, which cover practically the whole county, and a walking tour of Sligo City. On each of the driving tours there are a number of options for short walks along a wide variety of trails - from empty stretches of beach to secluded lakeshore woodlands. Each route has a different theme focusing on a specific or general highlight of that particular tour. We hope you enjoy the wonders of Sligo - whether young or old, active or passive, Sligo is the Land of Heart's Desire.

Fáilte go Contae Shligigh

Ó bharra na gcnoc go dtí an fharraige síos tá an ceanntar ar fad breachtha le radharcanna éagsúla agus iontaisí gan cuimse. Cé gur contae beag í tá sí lán le hachmhainní nádúrtha agus le muintir atá fial agus fáilteach. Chomh maith le sin tá ceol tradisúnta Shligigh molta go hard ar fud an domhain. Tá tabhacht idirnáisiúnta ag baint le séadchomharthaí an Chontae. Tá níos mó ná cúig mhíle láithreacha seandálaíochta ó ré na gcloch síos go dtí an seachtú céad déag le feiceáil ar fud an chontae. Thug áileacht na duthaí chomh maith le béaloideas, miotaseolaíocht agus stair na háite ionsparáid do fhilí, d'ealainteoirí ceoltóirí agus scolairí le fada an lá. Tá an tionchar seo le sonrú go láidir, saothaír litríochta W.B. Yeats. "Land of Heart's Desire" a bhaist sé ar an taobh seo tíre.

Sé aidhm an leabhráin seo ná cabhrú leis an gcuairteoir tairbhe a bhaint as saoire sa chontae. Tá seacht roinn sa leabhrán sé chinn a thugann cúntas ar thurasanna timpeall an chontae agus an seachtá ceann dírithe ar shiúlóid sa gCathair. Sa leabhrán freisin tá neart rogha agat de thurasanna gearra agus siúlóidí eagsúla cois trá nó ar na cnoic nó ins na coillte cnómhara cois locha. Tá súil againn go mbainfidh tú taitneamh agus tairbhe as iontaisí Shligigh

Bienvenue à Sligo

Sligo est un comté tout en conrastes qui vous surprendra par la variété spectaculaire de ses paysages et de ses vues . Bien qu'il soit l'un des plus petits comtés d'Irlande, Sligo a tout pour combler les visiteurs; non seulement la grande beauté de ses paysages et la qualité de ses équipements, mais aussi la musique traditionnelle superbe, et la chaleur de ses habitants. C'est à Sligo que l'on trouve l'une des plus riches concentrations de monuments préhistoriques et plus tardifs de l'Europe occidentale avec plus de 5000 sites archéologiques répertoriés. La beauté de ses paysages et les mythes, légendes at histoire qui s'y rattachent ont fasciné poètes, artistes et érudits à travers les ages. C'est le lauréat irlandais du prix Nobel, William Butler Yeats le poète le plus inspiré par Sligo, qui l'a baptisé " Land of Heart's Desire" (Le Pays de vos Rêves).

Le but de cette brochure est de vous aider à profiter au maximum de votre visite à Sligo. Elle contient six circuits en voiture, qui couvrent pratiquement tout le comté, et une visite à pied de la ville de Sligo. Chaque circuit comporte un certain nombre de suggestions pour de courtes promenades le long d'une grande variété de sentiers - plages désertes comme bois secrets au bord d'un lac. Nous espérons que vous allez tous apprécier les merveilles de Sligo, quels que soient votre âge ou votre tempérament. Sligo est " Land of Heart's Desire" (Le Pays de vos Rêves).

Herzlich willkommen in Sligo!

Sligo ist eine Gegend mit überraschenden Widersprüchen und einer spektakulären Landschaft. Obwohl eine der kleineren Grafschaften, bietet Sligo alles, was man sich wünscht: Gute Einkaufs - und Unterhaltungsmöglichkeiten, freundliche Leute und ausgezeichnete traditionelle Musik. Trotz einer rasanten Entwicklung in den letzten Jahren, hat Sligo seinen natürlichen Reiz nicht verloren. Sie finden hier eine der reichhaltigsten Anzahl prähistorischer Stätten und archäologischer Monumente in Westeuropa, einige davon über 5000 Jahre alt. Die Schönheit der Landschaft mit ihrer faszinierenden Mischung von Mythen, Legenden und Geschichte ist innig verbunden mit herausragenden Dichtern, Malern und Gelehrten der jeweiligen Zeit. Die Arbeit des Dichters und Nobelpreisträgers William Butler Yeats hatte sicher den größten Einfluß auf Sligo. Er nannte es 'the Land of Heart's Desire', das Land meiner Herzenswünsche.

Dieses Büchlein soll Ihnen helfen, das meiste aus Ihrem Aufenthalt in Sligo zu machen. Es enthält sechs Rundfahrten, die sie praktisch die gesamte Grafschaft entdecken lassen und eine Stadtbesichtigung von Sligo. Bei jeder Tour gibt es eine Reihe von Möglichkeiten für kurze Abstecher zu einsamen Stränden oder abgelegenen Wäldern an Seen. Entdecken und genießen Sie die 'Wunder' von Sligo und vielleicht wird es ja das Land *Ihrer* Herzenswünsche.

Benvenuti a Sligo

Sligo è una terra di sorprendenti contrasti, con una spettacolare varietà di viste e paesaggi. Una delle più piccole contee d'Irlanda, Sligo contiene tutto ciò che si potrebbe desiderare; non solo le numerosissime e variegate attrattive e bellezze naturali, ma anche la splendida musica tradizionale e il calore della sua gente. Sligo ha una delle più ricche concentrazioni di monumenti preistorici e più tardi dell'Europa occidentale, con più di 5.000 siti archeologici registrati. La bellezza della campagna e l'affascinante miscela di mito, leggenda e storia che la circonda hanno affascinato da sempre poeti, artisti e studiosi. L'influenza più notevole l'ha avuta sulle opere del poeta irlandese e premio Nobel William Butler Yeats, che chiamò Sligo "Land of Heart's Desire" *(La terra dei desideri del cuore)*.

Questo opuscolo si propone di aiutarvi a godere pienamente una visita a Sligo. Comprende sei gite in auto che coprono praticamente l'intera contea e una visita a piedi alla città di Sligo. Ognuna delle gite in auto contiene numerose opzioni per brevi passeggiate su percorsi diversi, da spiagge deserte a boschetti appartati sulle rive di un lago. Ci auguriamo che apprezzerete le meraviglie di Sligo: vecchi o giovani, sportivi o contemplativi, Sligo è sempre la "Land of Heart's Desire".

Bienvenidos a Sligo

Sligo es una tierra de sorprendentes contrastes con una variedad espectacular de paisajes. Aún siendo uno de los condados más pequeños de Irlanda, Sligo tiene todo lo que una persona pueda desear; no solo por la enorme variedad de encantos naturales y de amenidades que ofrece, sino también por su magnífica música tradicional y por la amabilidad de su gente. Sligo tiene una de las concentraciones más ricas de monumentos prehistóricos y de épocas posteriores de Europa occidental, con más de 5.000 lugares arqueológicos registrados. La belleza de su paisaje junto con su fascinante mezcla de mitos, leyendas e historia han fascinado a poetas, artistas y eruditos a través de los tiempos. La influencia más notable se deja ver en la obra del poeta William Butler Yeats, ganador del Premio Nobel para Irlanda que llamó a Sligo " The Land of Heart's Desire" (La Tierra que el Corazon desea).

El propósito de esto folleto es ayudarles a sacar el máximo partido de su visita a Sligo. Se indican seis excursiones para hacer en coche que cubren prácticamente la mayoría del condado y, un recorrido a pie de la ciudad de Sligo. En cada una de las rutas para hacer en coche se señalan un número de opciones para hacer pequeños recorridos andando por una amplia variedad de senderos que incluen desde tramos de playas desiertas hasta apartados bosques a las orillas de un lago. Esperamos que disfruten de las maravillas de Sligo - tanto para gente joven o vieja, activa o pasiva Sligo es la "Tierra que el Corazón desea". (The Land of Heart's Desire)

スライゴーにようこそ

　スライゴーは変化に富んだ素晴しい自然美が満ち溢れるこじんまりとした県の一つで、皆様がお求めになる全てのものが整っております。自然の魅力やレジャー設備の豊富さのみに限らず、素晴しい伝統的音楽や地元の人々の心暖まる歓待が待ち受けています。スライゴーは西ヨーロッパの中で先史時代や古代の史跡が最も集積していることで有名な地域の一つで、5000以上の考古学的史跡が記録されています。多くの詩人、芸術家、学者達がその田園の自然美や神話、伝説、歴史が綾を為す土地柄に、絶えず魅了されてきました。その中で最も強い影響を与えてきたのはノーベル賞受賞者である詩人、ウイリアム・バットラー・イエーツによる名作であり、スライゴーは「羨望の地」であるとイエーツによって讃えられています。

　このパンフレットはスライゴーを訪問される皆様に快適な一時をお過ごしいただくための一助として作成されたもので、その中にはスライゴー県全体を網羅する六つのドライブコースとスライゴー市街の徒歩ツアーが盛込まれています。ドライブコースの中には数多くのハイキングコースの中から、人影もまばらな静かな海岸や人里離れた湖畔の林などの短距離コースもオプションとして載せてあります。「羨望の地」スライゴーで老いも若きも、行動派も受け身型の方々もこの地の魅力を思い切りお楽しみ下さい。

Driving in County Sligo

There are a total of seven tours to take you around the whole of County Sligo. After each of the tours there is a fold out map, which can be kept open to aid you with the directions. The directions are as concise as possible, but be wary of signposts that may have been accidentally turned the wrong direction! By following the directions in the guide, coupled with the maps, you should stay on the route.

Irish roads vary considerably in standard. On some of the tours in this guide you will be travelling on narrow third class roads, some with grass growing down the middle. Take care on these, as tractors or livestock are often encountered. Also, if parking on these roads, make sure you do not block access to fields or hinder other traffic. Another point to note is that the older signposts give distances in miles while the newer ones are in kilometres; though, these clearly say that the distance is metric.

Sligo City has parking restrictions. There are a number of free car-parks on the verge of the centre, but elsewhere parking is paid by purchasing parking discs that are available in most shops

A Note on the Short Walks included in this Guide

The short walks included with each driving tour are a selection of the many walks that can be explored in the County. Most are straight forward and easy, but some involve going to high ground or across uneven terrain. In most cases you should be prepared for Ireland's notoriously changeable weather and have some waterproof clothing. Boots are not essential as all the walks are on roads or paths. However, sensible footwear is advised.

If you wish to explore other routes for walking and touring, the Ordnance Survey Discovery Series of maps in 1:50000 scale are highly recommended. Sheets 16, 24 and 25 cover most

Carrowkeel

of the county, while the remainder is covered by sheets 32 and 33.

Two long distance National Way-marked walking routes go through County Sligo. The Sligo Way is 73 kilometres and links the Western Way from Mayo at Lough Talt and crosses the Ox Mountains to Dromahair in County Leitrim. The Arigna Miner's Way and Historical Trail is a circular walk going from Arigna around Lough Key into Boyle in County Roscommon, around Lough Arrow and the Bricklieve Mountains in County Sligo. It then goes into County Leitrim linking to the Leitrim Way and the Cavan Way. It is 143 kilometres in length. Sections of these walks can be done and both have well produced guide books to accompany them. A total of 24 walks has been produced by communities between Ballintogher and Lough Talt to accompany the Sligo Way route. These are available locally in a specially produced pack.

Slí Stairiúil
HISTORICAL TRAIL

For other walks and tours enquire locally or contact:
North West Tourism Office
Temple Street
Sligo
Tel.. 071 61201

When touring please remember the following:

* Respect farmland and the rural environment.
* Guard against all risk of fire, especially near forests.
* Leave all farm gates as you find them.
* Always keep children under close control and supervision.
* Avoid entering farmland containing livestock.
* Do not enter farmland if you have dogs with you.
* Always use gates and stiles and avoid damage to walls, fences, etc.
* Take all your litter home.
* Take care on country roads.
* Protect wildlife, plants and trees.
* Do not block farm entrances when parking.
* Do not interfere with archaeological and national monuments in any way.

Note: **The Yeats Country Tour and the Ox Mountains Tour are two existing signposted driving routes. Sections of these are on some of the tours in this book. For further information on these specific drives see the book "Touring Sligo" by North West Tourism.**

Sligo - Naturally

It is not surprising that, given the wide range of landscapes in Sligo, many distinctive and varied habitats can be found. Coastal cliffs and dunes; lakes and rivers; bog and fen; mountains and valleys; karst and caves; estuaries and callows are some of the types of habitat which support the diverse and rich wildlife of the county.

Benbulben and Lough Gill have received considerable attention from naturalists. The cliffs of the limestone mountains of the Dartry Range, in particular those on the northern slopes, possess examples of arctic-alpine flowers and ferns. Peregrines, ravens and chough occur, along with other upland birds. Lough Gill supports a number of rare and uncommon plants such as the strawberry tree (see pg. 31). Uncommon butterflies and moths can be seen at places like Slish Wood, Ballygawley Lough, and other deciduous woodland areas.

The metamorphic rocks of the Ox Mountains are covered in extensive areas of blanket bog with intermittent expanses of exposed bare rock. The heather covered moorland of the mountains here support many birds of prey along with red grouse and other upland birds.

West and east of Lough Arrow are the limestone areas of the Bricklieve Mountains, Moytirra plateau around Highwood and Carran Hill. In the area around Highwood and in parts of the Bricklieves many beautiful orchids can be seen. Lough Arrow, Lough Gara and Templehouse Lake are large lakes that attract a variety of waterfowl. Lough Gara in particular has a large flock of wintering white fronted geese and also attracts whooper swans.

The coastal areas have an impressive and diverse range of seabird breeding areas. Ireland's most significant site for wintering barnacle geese is found at Lissadell. Inishmurray and Aughris head are two notable breeding areas. The dunes on the coast are also important habitats and many orchids occur. A substantial seal colony exists on the sand banks of Ballysadare Bay.

Peregrine Falcon

It is vital that all of these habitats are conserved and it is essential that when visiting any of these places that flora, fauna or habitat are not disturbed.

William Butler Yeats

William Butler Yeats, one of Ireland's most celebrated poets, was born in Dublin in 1865. He was not just absorbed in poetry and drama, but was a student and teacher of folklore, a mythologist, an historian, and an enthusiast of theosophy and related mystical interests. Besides these and other private enterprises he was an immensely energetic public figure; a journalist, literary critic, an impresario, a nationalist politician and a public speaker. He became a Free State senator for six years.

His father - John Butler Yeats - married Susan Mary Pollexfen, from Sligo, on 10 September 1863 in St John's Cathedral in Sligo. Because of this tie, William Butler, and his brother Jack spent much of their childhood and youth in this county. In his *Reveries over Childhood and Youth*, a collection of autobiographical pieces written in his forties, Yeats recalls the special people, times and places he experienced in Sligo. It gave him a sense of home and acceptance and, perhaps more importantly, it instilled in him a deep sense of appreciation of the landscape and of the folktales about that landscape. To him it was full of magic, of tales of danger and mystery which were part of daily life for the Sligo countrypeople.

This powerful and mysterious sense of place that he absorbed from the Sligo landscape emerges most prominently in his earliest works, but remained with him throughout his life. Sligo fed his growing need to find a sense of mystery and wonder - a sense of the sacred - that lay behind the immediate material reality of life. The world of the Faery - *the Sidhe* - entered much of his work and became a recurring theme that displayed the seriousness of many Irish folktales - life's dangerousness, precariousness, the pathos of human loss. Drumcliff Church in County Sligo became his final place of rest. He was buried there in 1948 after his body was removed from France, where he died in 1939.

Sligo City Walking Tour
Sligeach - the Place of Shells

This walking tour takes in most of the historical buildings and points of interest in Sligo. This tour can be done in a morning and then the 'Two Bird Mountain Tour' could be driven in the afternoon.

		Page
1	Tourist Information Centre	10
2	The Cathedral of the Immaculate Conception	10
3	St John's Cathedral	11
4	Harmony Hill	12
5	'The Friary'	13
6	Old Market Street	13
7	Teeling Street and Sligo Courthouse	13
8	'The Abbey'	14
9	Garavogue River	15
10	Calry Church	15
11	Niland Model Centre	16
12	The Green Fort	17
13	Stephen Street	17
14	Yeats Memorial Building	19
15	Wine Street	19
16	City Hall	19
17	Famine Memorial	20
18	Methodist Church	20
19	'Western Wholesale Company'	20

Driving Tours and Short Walks in County Sligo

The map opposite shows the County of Sligo and surrounding areas. It has all the main roads marked (primary routes in green and secondary roads in orange) and shows the different tours in this guide (apart from the walking tour of Sligo City). The key to the tours is below with the page number that they face.

The maps are designed so that they can be kept open while touring, and the directions and details of the tour highlights can be read with the maps. Detours are marked the same as the main tour on the map but are differentiated in the narrative. Third class roads (in yellow) are marked on each map to avoid confusion.

Map

Two Bird Mountain Tour — Page 32
A Circuit of Lough Gill

The Boar of Benbulben Tour — Page 33
A Tour of Yeat's Country and North County Sligo

Queen Maeve Tour — Page 56
A Tour of the Coolera peninsula, the Eastern Ox Mountains and the coast to Aughris Head

The Labby Tour — Page 57
A Drive around the Lough Arrow Region

The Bardic Tour — Page 80
A Tour through the Ox Mountains and the northern Coastline of Tireragh Baroney

The Corran Tour — Page 81
A Tour of Ballymote, Gurteen and Lough Gara in South County Sligo.

Walks

These are marked on each successive map as a solid thin red line. Walks are indicated next to highlights when they occur on the tour.

SLIGO

land of heart's desire

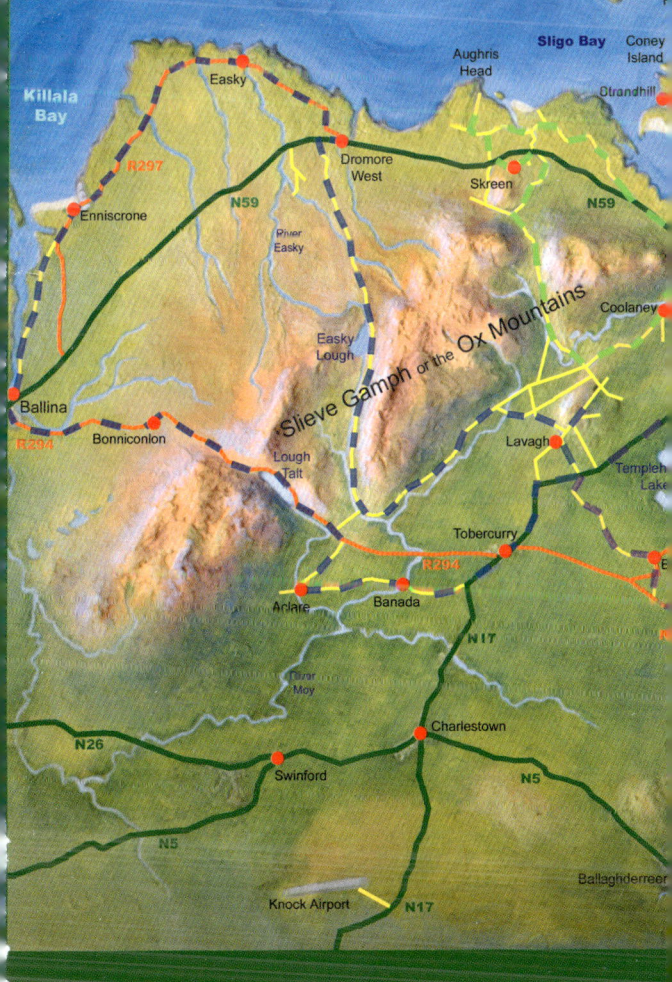

Atlantic Ocean

Inishmurray Island

Sligo Bay
Coney Island
Strandhill
Aughris Head
Killala Bay
Easky
R297
Dromore West
Skreen
N59
Enniscrone
River Easky
N59
Easky Lough
Coolaney
Slieve Gamph or the Ox Mountains
Ballina
R294
Bonniconlon
Lough Talt
Lavagh
Templehouse Lake
Tobercurry
R294
Aclare
Banada
N17
River Moy
N26
Charlestown
Swinford
N5
N5
Ballaghaderreen
Knock Airport
N17

Sligo City Walking Tour

Donegal Bay
Mullaghmore
Bundoran
N15
Kinlough
Duff River
Lough Melvin
Garrison
Cliffoney
Grange
R280
Truskmore
N15
Benbulben
Glencar
Dough Mountain
Drumcliff
Point
Lugnagall
N16
N16
Manorhamilton
Keelogyboy
Benbo
SLIGO
R292
R286
R280
Lough Gill
Dromahair
R287
R289
Ballysadare
Collooney
R284
Drumkeeran
Owenmore River
River Unshin
N17
N4
Riverstown
Lough Allen
R293
R280
Corry Mountain
Ballymote
Geevagh
Castlebaldwin
Ballyfarnon
Keash
R284
Lough Arrow
Bricklieve Mountains
Keadue
R293
Curlew Mts
Lough Key
Gurteen
Boyle
Lough Gara
Boyle River
N4
Monasteraden
Carrick-on-Shannon
R293
River Shannon
N61

Boar of Benbulben Tour & N15

Garavogue River

Maeve Tour & Strandhill

Dublin & N4

Sligo City Walking Tour
Sligeach - the Place of Shells

Rockwood Parade

The Place of Shells

Sligo's name - 'the Place of Shells' comes from the fact that there was an abundance of shellfish found at the river and estuary - the river was also called the Sligeach (now called the Garavogue River). The Ordnance Survey letters of 1836 state that 'cart loads of shells were found underground in many places within the town where houses now stand.' This whole area, from the river estuary of the 'Shelly River', around the coast to the river at Ballysadare Bay, was rich in marine resources and was a prime reason for large settlement of the region during the prehistoric period. Fishing, hunting seals, and the gathering of large quantities of seashell were probably regular activities of prehistoric and later settlers of the area.

Sligo City is the largest urban area in the North West and has a population of over 17,000. It is one of the most beautifully situated towns in Ireland. The city is located on the banks of the Garavogue River with Sligo Bay, the Coolera peninsula and Knocknarea to the west, Lough Gill to the East; the Ox Mountains to the south; and the Dartry Mountains, and the striking outline of Benbulben to the north. It is well situated for touring the varied and beautiful landscapes in the surrounding countryside as well as being ideal for travelling to neighbouring counties. It has all the amenities and services needed by the visitor; art galleries, theatres, cinema, museum, excellent shops, restaurants and pubs, great traditional music and many links with the poet W.B. Yeats and his brother, Jack B. Yeats.

Brief History of Sligo City

The development of Sligo as a town stemmed from its strategic location between Lough Gill and the sea, and it was always considered the gateway from the

Sligo Dominican Friary

province of Connacht into Ulster. It rose to prominence with the Anglo Norman invasion of Connacht in 1235, although there are records of settlement and the existence of a bridge prior to this. A castle was built in 1245 and a Dominican Friary was founded in 1252-53. In 1310 a new castle was built and a new town laid out by Richard III de Burgo, the Red Earl of Ulster. This castle was destroyed in 1315 by the O'Donnells. O'Connor Sligo then had effective control of the town throughout the 14th century. In the 15th and 16th centuries the town's prosperity owed much to the proximity of the herring shoals. The later wars of the 16th century, principally between the O'Neills and the O'Donnells against Queen Elizabeth I, devastated the town. However, after 1603 and the end of the wars, the settlement began to prosper once again. In 1641 the town and Friary were sacked by the Parliamentarian Sir Frederick Hamilton. In 1645 the town was captured by the Cromwellian Sir Charles Coote II. In 1689 it was seized by Williamite rebels under Lord Kingston, but was retaken by Patrick Sarsfield for King James. During the 18th and 19th centuries the town grew, as did the importance of the port of Sligo. It was incorporated as a town in 1612 and today Sligo is the commercial, cultural and educational centre of the North West.

Begin the tour outside North West Tourism Centre on Temple Street.

1 Tourist Information Centre
This modern building houses the Tourist Information Centre which services all visitor enquiries and provides accommodation reservations, a bureau de change, maps and guides (Tel. 071 61201). The County Sligo Genealogical Service is also located in this building, as is Sligo's renowned theatre - The Hawks Well (071 61526) - named after a play by William Butler Yeats, inspired by Tullaghan Well near Coolaney on the Queen Maeve Tour (see pg. 50).

A short walk northward along Temple Street brings you to the first stop

2 The Cathedral
The Cathedral of The Immaculate Conception was built in what has been called a Renaissance Romanesque style by the then Bishop of Elphin, Laurence Gillooly (1858-1895). Its architect was George Goldie. It was consecrated in 1874. One of the chief attractions of the Cathedral is the lighting effect of the 69 stained glass windows.

Sligo Cathedral

The first bishop of the Diocese of Elphin is said to be St Asicus, who was consecrated by St Patrick and was the saint's coppersmith. A replica of a statue found on Inishmurray Island, depicting St Molaise, is at the back of the nave near the door (see pg. 40). A small wooden statue of unknown date, also located at the back of the nave near the door, has been identified as St Asicus. On a plaque beside the statue is a copy of a page from the Book of Armagh, written in 807 AD, concerning the life of St Patrick and St Asicus' name is mentioned many times. The altar and tabernacle of the cathedral are in beaten brass symbolically recalling the saint's work as a coppersmith. There are nine bells in the bell tower, which was erected in 1876, the largest of the bells being 1.5 tons.

At the main door of the Cathedral turn left and go through the car-park to John Street.

3 St John's Cathedral

This road takes its name from the Church of Ireland Cathedral - the Cathedral of St John the Baptist. This church is probably on the site of an Anglo-Norman 'hospital' or Alms House built in 1242 AD. In 1637 Sir Roger Jones of Banada, Governor of Sligo, had a mortuary chapel built here. The top slab of his tomb was discovered during the alterations to the church in 1812 and this is now found on the west wall. In 1730 the famous German architect, Richard Cassels, came to Sligo to build Hazelwood House (see pg. 30), and was also commissioned to redesign this church. His other notable buildings in Ireland are Leinster House, the Rotunda, and Powerscourt. Many of Cassel's design features were lost during changes to the building in 1812 and 1883 when gothic features replaced his work.

St John's Cathedral

On the wall of the northern transept, near the pulpit, there is a brass plaque to the memory of Susan Mary Yeats who died in London in 1900. She was William Pollexfen's eldest daughter who, on 10 September 1863, married John Butler Yeats in this church. They became the parents of William Butler and Jack Butler Yeats. W.B. Yeats' grandfather, William Pollexfen and his wife were laid to rest here in 1892. George Pollexfen, uncle to Jack and William Butler Yeats, was also buried here in 1910.

The Cholera Epidemic of 1832, Charlotte Thornley, and "Dracula"

Near the south west wall of St John's Cathedral is the Thornley family burial plot. This name has interesting associations with both the cholera epidemic in Sligo in 1832 and with Dracula.

Both of Bram Stoker's biographers, Harry Ludlam and Daniel Farson, agree that it was the tales his mother re-told to the young Stoker, which inspired him in later life to write his famous novel - "Dracula". Stoker's gothic novel was published only 55 years after his mother Mrs. Charlotte Stoker, witnessed horrific scenes on the streets of her native Sligo. A daughter of Lieut. Thomas Thornley, her family lived in Sligo during most of the cholera epidemic.

The dreadful disease, which struck hardest in August 1832, was responsible for many deaths. The illness caused some people to slip into an unconscious state; these were often pronounced dead. Perhaps one of the most gruesome of tales surrounding the disease, related by Charlotte Stoker in her memoirs, is that of a former soldier known as 'Long Sergeant Callen'. He was a man of great stature who contracted cholera and was presumed dead. The coffin makers based in Sligo's old Courthouse were mass producing coffins of a fixed size; too short for the sergeant. When they found he would not fit they took a hammer to break his legs to make him fit. However, the first blows violently woke the sergeant from his unconscious state. He later made a full recovery from the disease.

Presbyterian Church

Continue down John Street and take the next right into Charles Street. Turn left at the top on to Church Street. On the corner of Church Street is the Presbyterian Church, built in 1828. Cross the next road encountered, Harmony Hill, which goes down to the left. Proceed straight across to the narrow road called West Gardens.

4 Harmony Hill
Local folklore says that the origin of the name Harmony Hill stemmed from faction fighting between different families who

washed in the Garavogue River. The river was used as a laundry place and proximity to the best sites on washing days was much sought after. Rows often broke out between families converging near the river. However, when this hill was constructed as a road, it meant that families could get to the river without coming into conflict with one another, thus restoring the town's harmony! Its old name was Waste Water Lane and this led to Waste Gardens, the correct name for the street you are now walking down - West Gardens - as this was originally a refuse site for the town in the days of old!

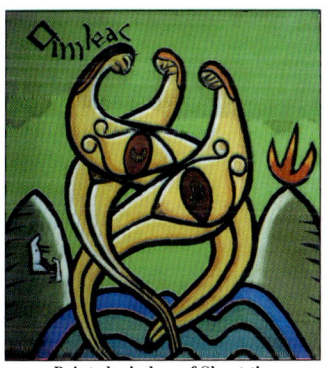

Painted window of Shoot the Crows Pub at the bottom of Market Street

From West Gardens turn right on to High Street. To the left is Market Street

5 'The Friary'

High Street was part of the old south road out of Sligo, once containing many inns and hotels. The most notable building on High Street is the Church of the Dominican Order, commonly called 'the Friary'. Designed by Pearse McKenna in 1973 the modern building replaced a church of 1845, the apse of which is still preserved with a two light window (1911) portraying St Raymundus and St Antonius.

Take the left branch off at the end of High Street on to Old Market Street.

6 Old Market Street

The most prominent name on this street was Peter O'Connor, general merchant and timber importer, who paid for the bells in Sligo's Cathedral. On March 15th 1846 he placed an advert announcing the departure of a ship from Sligo's port bound for Quebec and thence to New York. This marked the start of the great exodus from Ireland's shores during the potato famine. By the following year over 13,000 people sailed from the port of Sligo.

Turn left at the end of Old Market Street on to Teeling Street.

7 Teeling Street & Courthouse

At the end of Old Market Street one comes to the Courthouse, built in 1878. The exterior is extremely gothic and has some features that were modelled on the Law Courts of London.

Courthouse

This street is named after Bartholomew Teeling, a hero of the 1798 rebellion (see pg. 54). Across the road are the former offices of a uniquely named professional partnership - Argue and Phibbs Solicitors! Its name featured in articles in Ripley's 'Believe It or Not', and in the satirical magazine 'Punch'. Mr W.H. Argue and Mr Talbot Phibbs' firm ended in 1944, yet its name is preserved on the plaque and window of the present day solicitors.

After passing the Courthouse, take the next right turn on to Abbey Street

8 The Abbey

This takes you to Sligo's only surviving medieval building - Sligo's Dominican Friary, founded in 1252/3 by Maurice Fitzgerald, Chief Justice of Ireland. Most people in Sligo call this building 'the Abbey'. The eight lancet windows on the south side of the choir were built in the 13th century. Two of these windows are blocked - one by the 15th century tower and rood screen; the other by the insertion of the O'Connor Sligo memorial dated 1624. The sacristy and chapter house date from the 13th century, but the cloister and remaining buildings were added about two centuries later.

Despite an accidental fire in 1414 and damage during a siege of Sligo Castle during the Elizabethan period the Friary remained intact. However, on July 1st 1642 it was sacked by Sir Frederick Hamilton and his Puritan soldiers; the friars were massacred and the building was left as a ruin. The remaining structure is in good condition, with many of the tombs, monuments and features retaining much of their original splendour. It has the oldest decorated high altar in an Irish monastic church, dating probably to the 15th century, and the beautifully carved O'Crean tomb dating to 1506 is an example of a medieval grave monument. A legend persists that the silver bell of the Friary lies at the bottom of Lough Gill and only the purest of souls are privileged to hear it when it rings out.

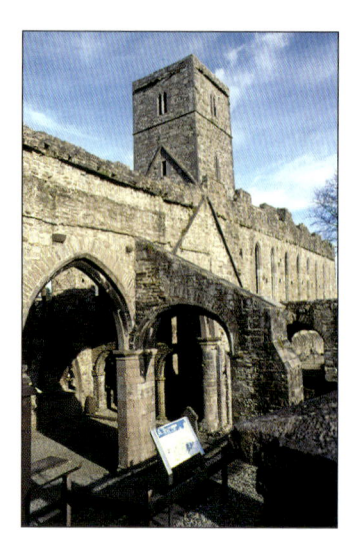

Sligo Dominican Friary is under state care and managed through Dúchas, the Heritage Service.

Opening Times
Daily   mid-June - mid-Sept.
        09.30-18.30.
Tel.   071 46406.

At other times the keys can be obtained from the caretaker: Mr Anthony McQuinn, 6 Charlotte Street, (around the corner to the right of Abbey Street)

Dipper on the Garavogue

On leaving the Friary turn left and follow the road to the left on to Lower Abbey Street which comes out by the river on to John F. Kennedy Parade. Turn right along the Riverside as far as the pedestrian bridge and cross the River Garavogue to continue the tour. Otherwise a pleasant walk along the banks of the river can be enjoyed by proceeding to Doorly Park, which contains an interesting nature trail and fine views along the river (see pg. 22).

9 Garavogue River

On crossing the river look in the water below for signs of salmon. The salmon season is very long in these waters. An ancient manuscript telling the life of St Patrick states that the saint encountered two fishermen here and asked them for a salmon. They informed the saint that salmon were not in this river during the winter, but that they would do as he desired and cast their nets. To their surprise they caught a large salmon and presented it to Patrick. In return

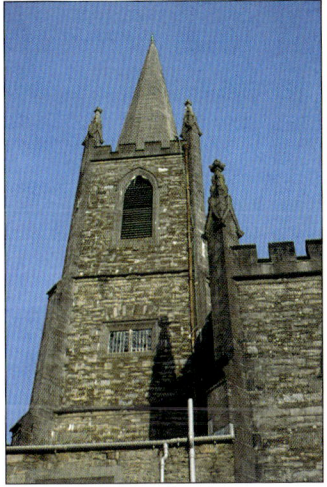

Calry Church

he blessed the river and imparted to it the privilege of yielding salmon all year round.

Proceed up the lane towards the Mall and Calry Church.

10 Calry Church

Calry Church was completed in 1824 to accommodate the growing Church of Ireland population in Sligo town and surroundings. Considerable improvement works were carried out in 1885. One of these involved the erection of a hydraulic engine to replace manual labour involved in working the church's organ.

Fishing on the Garavogue

Model Niland Centre

Proceed down the Mall towards the centre of Sligo City

11 Niland Model Centre

On the right hand side is a large building called the Model Niland Centre, the principle arts and cultural centre for the North West. It was built as a 'Model School' in 1862. As with other Model Schools established around that time it was instituted to provide instruction for children of different denominations, in the principle of combined secular and separate religious instruction.

Recently the building became the Model Arts Centre. It houses touring exhibitions and features a wide range of cultural activities within its walls including literary and music festivals. It is undergoing a two million pound refurbishment and is being extended to accommodate a purpose built exhibition space suitable for large touring exhibitions. It will also house the municipal collection, part of which is currently on show upstairs in Sligo City Library. This is a superb collection of modern Irish artists with many of the works being collected by Sligo's former head librarian and Yeats enthusiast, Nora Niland who died in 1988. It includes works by Paul Henry, Sean Keating, Maurice McGonigal, AE (George Russell), Nano Reid and John B. Yeats. It also has a large collection of the works of Jack Yeats. The new Model Niland Centre is officially to open in May 2000.

Jack B. Yeats

William Butler Yeats often complained that his young brother Jack had supplanted him in his Pollexfen grandparents' affections. In 1879 Jack didn't return to London with the family. Instead, he stayed in Sligo with his grandparents. He went to school in Sligo for the next eight years. Jack's grandparents allowed him every freedom and he moved amongst the people of Sligo and absorbed the magic of Sligo. Its mountains, its idyllic woods, its lakes, and most particularly, its ever-changing skies were to appear again and again in his future work. "Sligo was my school," he wrote, "and the sky above it."

Some of his pictures had a special significance for Jack Yeats, like the one illustrated here, that is called **'Leaving the Far Point'**. It commemorates a visit to Sligo with his wife, Mary Cottenham Yeats - known as Cottie - at some date between 1900 and 1910. It particularly commemorates a walk at Rosses Point with his uncle, George Pollexfen, who carries a stick, and with Cottie. Jack has included himself, wearing a wide-

The Green Fort

Leaving the Far Point by Jack B. Yeats 1946 (© Ann and Michael Yeats)

brimmed hat. This picture was of such sentimental value that he gave it to Cottie on her birthday in 1947. After her death it came back to him as part of her estate. In 1954 he presented it to the Mayor in the name of the citizens of Sligo. **'Leaving the Far Point'** is now part of the permanent collection of Yeats pictures currently on display in the Sligo Museum and Art Gallery in Stephen Street which will move on completion of the Model Niland Centre.

Continue down the Mall and turn right and up the hill to Connaughton Road. Turn right again, cross the road and a gate opposite the car-park brings one to the Green Fort. After going through the gate turn right and uphill towards an overgrown embankment.

12 The Green Fort

The fort's strategic location for artillery provides one of the finest views of the surrounding countryside. The Green Fort is an earthwork artillery fortification located on high ground to the north of the town, possibly dating to around 1646. Sligo town was extensively fortified during the Jacobite war and the Green Fort became the strongest part of the town's defences. The Jacobite commander, Sarsfield, constructed additional works at the Green Fort during the end of 1689. After the Jacobite defeat at the Battle of the Boyne in July 1690 Sir Teige O'Regan took command of Sligo. He held out against constant attacks from the Williamites until September 1691, the Green Fort having at that time a Jacobite garrison of 600 men and sixteen guns. The earthworks and bastions survive on the site today, but the earthworks constructed in 1689 are not evident.

Return the way you came, back to the junction of the Mall, Bridge Street, and Stephen Street. Turn right on to Stephen Street.

13 Stephen Street

The attractive building on the corner, the **AIB Bank**, formerly housed the Provincial Bank until the early 1970's. The Provincial

AIB Bank on Stephen Street

Bank was the first bank to open in Sligo in 1826. Among its first clients were many of the landed gentry of Sligo. The present Renaissance style building was erected in 1880.

The next building of note is again on the right of the street and contains **Sligo City Library and Museum.** The chapel was originally built in 1851 for the Independent Church along with its adjacent manse. In 1955 the museum opened in the manse. By 1958 a special section called the 'Yeats Memorial Museum' was established. It houses many of his literary works and also contains the Nobel Prize Medal awarded to Yeats.

There is a small collection of objects of national and local interest dating from prehistoric times to the Anglo-Irish War (1919-21). The large mural inside the library depicts the Battle of the Books at Cooldrumman (see pg. 36).

Until the refurbishment of the new Model Niland Centre is completed and opened in May 2000, part of the Municipal Art Collection is on display upstairs in the Library. Many of the works on show are by Jack Yeats.

Opening Times
April - May / Oct - Dec
Tues - Sat   14.00-16.50
Mid June -mid Sept
Mon - Sat   10.00-12.00
and   14.00-16.50

The Gallery keeps similar hours June to September, but is closed on Mondays. In April, May and October it is open in the morning only.

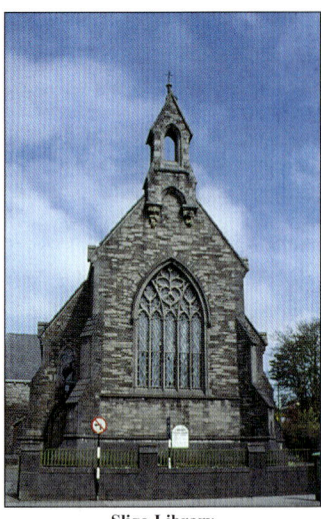

Sligo Library

Continue towards the River Garavogue

On the corner of Stephen Street and Markievicz Road is the **Ulster Bank**, built in 1863. When Yeats was in Stockholm to receive his Nobel Prize for Literature in 1923 he commented on the architecture of the Swedish Royal Palace saying that it reminded him somewhat of this Classical Renaissance building.

The **statue of William Butler Yeats** in front of the bank was sculpted by Rowan Gillespie and is engraved with lines from Yeats' own verses covering the torso. It was erected by public subscription to commemorate the fiftieth anniversary of the poet's death in 1989.

Cross Hyde Bridge and cross the road to the Yeats Memorial Building.

14 Yeats Memorial Building
The **Hyde Bridge** is named after Dr Douglas Hyde (1860-1949), the first president of the Irish Republic (see pg. 65). The first stone of the bridge was laid in 1846 and on its completion in 1852 it was named Victoria Bridge after the reigning English Queen. It replaced a bridge built in the middle of the 17th century. The Yeats Memorial Building was erected by the Belfast Banking Company in 1895. It became part of the Allied Irish Bank Group in 1970 and they donated it to the Yeats Society in 1973. It is now the centre for the Yeats International Summer School (071 42693), an annual gathering of international scholars and students of literature interested in the works of Yeats. The building also houses the **Sligo Art Gallery** (071 45847) with travelling and local artists' exhibitions and paintings. It is open weekdays 10.00-17.00, and on Saturday to 13.00. Across the road is a mural of W.B. Yeats with many scenes from his life and works.

To the left is O'Connell Street, Sligo's main shopping area. Continue straight and past the General Post Office, which was built in 1902 and on to Wine Street.

Statue of W.B. Yeats

Ulster Bank

15 Wine Street
Wine Street got its name from the wine vaults which the Bulteel family once had at the corner of this street and O'Connell Street. The store of Henry Lyons and Co. was opened here in 1878.

Turn right off Wine Street on to Quay Street to the City Hall.

16 City Hall
The foundation stone was laid by the then Lord Mayor, W.A. Woods, in October 1865. Built in a French Renaissance style the building is probably on the site of a Cromwellian stone fort, built in 1646. A statue of P.A. McHugh stands outside. He was the Nationalist owner of the 'Sligo Champion' newspaper. McHugh was elected Mayor of Sligo for five years in succession and

became a Member of Parliament for North Leitrim in 1892. He died in 1909. The statue was erected in 1916.

Continue down Quay Street to the car-park.

P.A. McHugh

Rockwood Parade & the Garavogue

17 Famine Memorial
This hauntingly powerful statue was erected in 1997 in memory of the tragedy of Ireland's Great Famine on the 150 year anniversary of the famine's worst year. The image of an emaciated father, mother and child huddled at the quayside evokes strong feelings. There is sorrow and sadness in the bowed parents, but a note of hope is evident in the figure of the child with her finger symbolically pointing to an on-coming ship that will take them all to a better life in the 'New World'. (Also see pg. 32)

Retrace your steps back to Wine Street and turn right

18 Methodist Church
The Methodist Chapel across the road from the Gaiety Cinema is called Wesley Chapel. As far back as 1775 the Methodists had a chapel in Sligo on Bridge Street. This building was opened in 1832. Between 1758 and 1789 John Wesley, the founder of the religion, visited Sligo 14 times.

On the other side of the road slightly further on are the offices of the Sligo Champion newspaper. The first issue, consisting of four pages, came out on June 4th 1836 and carried the motto 'Truth Conquers'.

Turn left at the end of Wine Street on to Adelaide Street.

19 Western Wholesale Company
On the corner here is the impressive stone building of the former Western Wholesale Company. This was once part of the extensive property of the Pollexfen family. On the roof can be seen the turret from which William Pollexfen, grandfather to William Butler Yeats, trained a telescope on his ships going in and out of port. During the 19th century the Middleton and Pollexfen family became the largest ship owners in Sligo. However, the busy port of Sligo gradually gave way to the arrival of the railway which opened on December 3 1862. By the 1890's the Middleton-Pollexfen Shipping Line had one small schooner left and by the end of the century it too had gone.

Continue along Adelaide Street and back to the beginning of the tour.

Famine Statue on Quay Street

Two Bird Mountain Tour

A Circuit of Lough Gill

Two Bird Mountain Tour

Slieve Daene is a mountain on the south western side of Lough Gill, and is part of the eastern end of the Ox Mountain chain. Its name means 'Mountain of the Two Birds', and on its northern slopes there is a small lake called Loch Dagee, 'Lake of the Two Geese'. Also, on an adjoining mountain to the west, Slieve Dargan there is a cairn of stones called 'Cailleach a Vera's House'. These are all tied together in a legend concerning the Cailleach, who in reality is the widely known Hag of Beare.

William Butler Yeats tells us in a note on 'The Dreaming of the Sidhe' that "the hag sought the deepest water in the world to drown her fairy nature, of which she had become dissatisfied".

Another version relates the story of Mad MacSweeny. This man was cursed by a monk, called Ronan, after MacSweeny attacked him and threw his holy bell into a lake. The curse caused MacSweeny to go mad and to believe he was a bird. He lived in trees and travelled around Ireland. After some time his relatives found him and brought him home where he began to recover from his madness.

However, one day an old woman challenged him to a jumping contest to which he agreed. The woman was none other than the hag. The two jumped from mountain-top to mountain-top and the hag could never better MacSweeny's leaps. She then challenged him to a diving contest and turned herself into a goose on Two Birds Mountain near to her house. MacSweeny dived into a small but very deep lake, Lough Dagee, so deep that its bottom reached the limits of hell. He re-surfaced and the hag leapt in and was never seen again. MacSweeny's insanity returned and he continued living in trees as a bird.

Doorly Park

Starting at the junction of Bridge Street and John F. Kennedy Parade - follow the River Garavogue heading east along the Riverside for 1 mile (1.6 km). Car-park is on the left hand side.

1 Garavogue River & Doorly Park

This beautiful spot close to Sligo City marks the end of a nature trail and is on a linear walk along the banks of the River Garavogue. This short river drains a water catchment covering an area of almost 400 km^2. The water quality is so good that it complies with the most stringent of water quality regulations. Doorly Park was named after a late Bishop of Elphin, Dr. Edward Doorly, but much of its natural diversity was formed in the 19th century by the owner of the land, the well known antiquary and historian, Colonel W.G. Wood-Martin. Through great ingenuity he developed the wetlands of his estate, called Cleaveragh and formed the unusual combination of a woodland canopy with a marshy wetland type ecology beneath. Many species of plants and wildlife can be appreciated.

Continue along the road for 1.5 miles (2.4 km) passing the Sligo Regional Sports Centre (on right) and turning left at T-junction. Views over the Garavogue River on left. Car-park for Carns Forest (easy to miss) on right.

2 Carns Forest

This is a pleasant forest walk on the outskirts of Sligo City and overlooks Lough Gill. The forest walk is 1 km long. In the middle of the forest, on the highest part of the hill, now fairly overgrown and difficult to find, is a cairn of stones, probably covering an ancient passage tomb. On an adjoining hill to the west is another cairn.

One of the legends concerning the cairns says that they are the burial places of two warriors called Romra and Omra. Romra had a beautiful daughter called Gile. One day she was bathing at Tobernalt when Omra saw her and was spellbound by her beauty. Romra discovered them together and declared war against Omra. Both died during the ensuing conflict and Gile's tears of grief caused the formation of the lake named after her - Lough Gill - meaning 'Bright Lake'.

Detour:

Continuing on from Carns Forest take the first turn right to a spectacular viewing point of Lough Gill at the water treatment plant on the top of the hill. Turn your car and return to the road, turning right to continue the tour

Continue along the road again for 1.1 miles (1.7 km). Just off the road to the right is Tobernalt Holy Well which is signposted.

View from detour.

3 Tobernalt Holy Well

This tranquil and beautifully peaceful place is maintained by locals and is a well-known place of pilgrimage. The principal pilgrimage day is the last Sunday of July known as Garland Sunday. A large rock in front of the well is said to have been used as an altar during the Penal Laws (see pg. 77). St Patrick is said to have prayed at the rock and pilgrims place their fingertips into indentations on its surface that are said to mark where the saint touched it. Pilgrims also rest their backs against the rock to obtain cures for backaches. The water from the well is said to have cures for eyesight and headaches. The 'Rag Tree', a holly bush near the statues of Calvary, is where pilgrims unburden ills and leave petitions at the well in the form of rags or other items. Although the altar, grottoes and stations are modern and the Church encourages the pilgrimage today, this well dates back to pagan times and many of the rituals performed today come from a pre-Christian era. Garland Sunday itself marks the beginning of Lughnasa, the festival of the Celtic god of the harvest - Lugh.

From the Holy Well to the next stop at Dooney Rock is 1.5 miles. (2.4 km) Continue along the road you were on. Turn left at the first T-junction on to the R287 road to Dromahair. Dooney Rock car-park is on the left hand side in wood land, and is signposted.

4 Dooney Rock

When I play on my fiddle in Dooney,
Folk dance like a wave of the sea;
My cousin is priest in Kilvarnet
My brother in Mocharabuiee.

'The Fiddler of Dooney', the poem by W.B. Yeats, has made this spot famous and also provides the name for a well known annual traditional music contest in Sligo. In the 19th century it was well known by naturalists such as R. L. Praeger. The area contains several rare

Tobernalt Holy Well

and uncommon plants, along with very interesting geology. A 1.2 km nature trail that forms a loop and begins and ends at the car-park is a pleasant and very interesting stroll. The most impressive part of the trail is the views from Dooney Rock itself. This involves a steep walk to the top of the rock. There was a cashel or stone fort here at one time. Dooney Rock comes from the Irish for the place - *Carraig Dhún Aodh* - meaning the Rock of the Fort of Hugh.

Berries of the spindle bush

The island nearest this viewing point is known as Cottage Island or Gallagher's Island, but everyone in Sligo calls it **Beezie's Island.** It was named after a much loved and hospitable Sligo character, called Beezie Gallagher, who lived on the island. She regularly rowed from her home into Sligo Town until her death in 1951.

Geology of this area

The Ox Mountains are made of 600 million year old metamorphic rock composed of gneiss. The road at Dooney Rock is on a fault line- a line of weakness where two pieces of land may have collided with one another. This fault separates the Ox Mountains gneisses and the Dartry limestone as it cuts through to the base of the earth's crust some 30 km below. The Dartry limestone makes up the carboniferous mountains on the north side of the lake, which are about 300 million years old.

Follow along on the R287 for 1.5 miles, (2.4 km) skirting the edge of Lough Gill. Slish Wood is on the left after the road curves to the south along an inlet. The entrance is signposted but is easy to miss.

5 Slish Wood

Where dips the rocky highland Of Sleuth Wood in the lake.

W.B.Yeats gave this place a slightly different name in his poem 'The Stolen Child', calling it Sleuth Wood. Much of the wood that had survived previous centuries was cleared during the Emergency Years of World War II, however, a fringe of the old wood - 250 years old - still remains along the lake shore.

Walks

There are a variety of walks that can be made here. Two are described here. Part of the Sligo Way, a long distance way marked trail, goes through here. The linear path can be followed to the east as far as Inishfree Island and a return trip made.

Young red deer at Slish Wood

Lough Gill from Dooney Rock Nature Trail

Otherwise a circular walk can be made of 3.5 km. From the car-park head east, towards the lake and follow the path for 2 km where the path rises from the shore. Take the first fork right. The slopes of Kilerry mountain are to the left. Continue until the T-junction on the path near the car-park, and turn left for it.

Follow the R287 for 1.4 miles (2.2 km) to a crossroads. Go straight across here, following the signs for Castleore Stone Fort. 300 m from the crossroads is a narrow lane to the left which leads to a small car-park, from which there is a 10 minute walk to the cashel.

6 Castleore Stone Fort

This is an excellent example of a cashel or stone fort. It is also called Cashel Bir. It is 23m in diameter and the walls are 2.8m thick. Many cashels exist in the county and impressive examples such as this one may have been a symbol of social, rather than military prestige. Most belong to the Early Christian period (440-1200 AD), but some excavated examples have dated back to earlier periods.

Castleore Stone Fort

Return to the crossroads and the R287 and turn right towards Dromahair. After 2 miles (3.2 km) turn left down a narrow road signposted to Innisfree Island. After 0.8 miles (1.3 km) park at Killery graveyard on the left. The road is narrow so park in a way that other road users can pass.

7 Killery Straining Thread

Almost hidden amongst the tomb stones, slightly to the right of the entrance, is a collection of seven egg-shaped stones around a small rectangular stone, with pieces of thread and string tied around it. This 'straining string' supposedly possesses an infallible cure for all manner of pains, aches and strains. The sufferer, or a deputy, removes from the 'straining

Kilerry Straining Stones

stone' a piece of string, replacing it with another string. They then take each stone in succession and repeat certain prayers whilst turning it. A 19th century historian called the practice "one of the most perfect representations of the survival of the semi-Christianisation of a pagan custom".

Continue along the road following signs to Innisfree for 2 miles (3.2 km) until a small car-park is reached. The viewing point to the island is 100 m further on.

8 Innisfree Island

I will arise and go now, go to Innisfree,
And a small cabin build there of clay and wattles made:
Nine bean-rows will I have there, a hive for the honey bee,
And live alone in the bee-loud glade.

'The Lake Isle of Innisfree' was immortalised by W.B.Yeats who tells us that: "My father had read me a passage out of Walden, and I planned to live some day in a cottage on a little island called Innisfree." There is a fine view from the shore here including Cloghereevagh House high on the other shore to the north west. Once owned by the Gore-Booth family, the house is now part of St Angela's College. Also visible is the mountainous profile of a 'Sleeping Giant' on the opposite shore in the Dartry Mountains.

Return to the R287 and turn left for Dromahair (4 miles (6.4 km) from Innisfree)

9 Dromahair, County Leitrim

On the left, as one enters the town is 'Old Hall' which adjoins the fragmentary remains of O'Rourke's Castle. It incorporates portions of a castle and bawn built in 1626 by Sir Edward Villiers, brother of the Duke of Buckingham and grantee of O'Rourke's lands. This whole area was the chief

Lough Gill sunset near Dromahair

seat of the O'Rourkes - the ancient kings of Breifne, an area of land that covered a considerable area of this region. The village itself was laid out by the English landlords of the area, the Lane-Foxes, who based it on a plan of a village in Somerset, England.

In Thomas Moore's song, 'The Valley Lay Smiling Before Me' based on this area, the tale is told of the famous elopement of Dervorgilla. She left her husband, Tigernan O'Rourke, King of Breifne, for Diarmat Mac Murrough, King of Leinster. His subsequent banishment provided Henry II with a pretext for the conquest of Ireland.

Walk

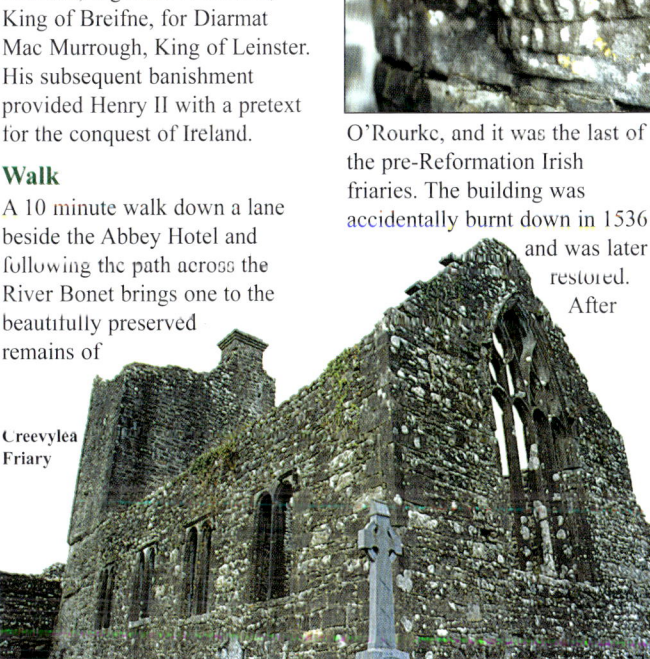

A 10 minute walk down a lane beside the Abbey Hotel and following the path across the River Bonet brings one to the beautifully preserved remains of

Creevlea Friary. This was a Franciscan establishment founded in 1508 by Margaret

St Francis

O'Rourke, and it was the last of the pre-Reformation Irish friaries. The building was accidentally burnt down in 1536 and was later restored. After

Creevylea Friary

Parke's Castle

banishment in the early 17th century, the friars returned on two occasions to re-occupy the building. On a column in the cloisters, carvings of St Francis can be found - one showing his stigmata, one showing him preaching to the birds.

Driving through Dromahair, on the R 288, there is a lay-by on the lakeshore after 3 miles (4.8 km) with a viewing point of Lough Gill. The road then meets the R286 where you continue straight for Parke's Castle a total of 5 miles (8 km) from Dromahair.

10 Parke's Castle, County Leitrim

This magnificently located fortified manor house at the eastern end of Lough Gill was built in 1609 by Captain Robert Parke, an English settler. It has been beautifully restored by the Office of Public Works using 17th century building techniques and native Irish oak. During the work the foundations of a tower house belonging to the O'Rourkes was unearthed. It is a fascinating place to visit, and guided tours are available along with an audio-visual presentation on other archaeological sites in County Sligo.

Opening Times:
14-17 March - Daily - 10.00-17.00
11 Apr-31 May
Tues-Sun - 10.00-17.00
June-Sept - Daily - 09.30-18.30
October - Daily - 10.00-17.00

Tel. 071 64149

Detour
Continuing on the R286 heading west from Parke's Castle take the right turn after 2 miles (3.2 km), signposted for Calry. Continue to the end of this narrow road to a T-junction and turn left. 300m further, turn left into a car-park - sign posted for Giant's Graves and Deerpark.

11 Deerpark

This forest was formally the walled area where the Wynne family of Hazelwood kept their deer herd for hunting (see pg. 30) and is now a state owned forest. A number of walks can

Lough Colgagh

be taken through the wood here but the main attraction of the area is its archaeology. An undulating path, mainly uphill and steep in places, is sign posted from the car-park. This leads to the Central Court Tomb on top of a hill, which dates to the Neolithic Period or New Stone Age - *c*4000-2500 BC. Its most distinctive feature is the open court at the centre which appears to have been a place used for ritual, and which provided access to the galleries. This particular example is considered by many to be the finest example of such a monument in the country. Made of rough limestone it consists of an oval gallery 15m long with two galleries on the eastern end and one to the western end. Large lintel stones once spanned the entrances to the galleries but only one survives, this being split in two and in danger of falling. In the 19th century, exploratory excavations uncovered human and animal bones, mainly those of deer.

From the detour return to the R286 and turning right follow directions below.

Continue along the R286 for 7 miles (11.3km). A lay-by on the right over-looks Lough Colgagh. It is worth

Deerpark Court Tomb

stopping here for the fine view of the Dartry mountains framing the lake with Deerpark forest above it.

Another 3 miles (4.8 km) on, passing Calry football grounds, turn left for Hazelwood - sign posted. Turn left at sign post for forest/ picnic site. The car-park is at the end of this road.

12 Hazelwood

Hazelwood

I went out to the hazel wood,
Because a fire was in my head,
And cut and peeled a hazel wand,
And hooked a berry to a thread;
And when white moths were on the wing,
And moth-like stars were flickering out,
I dropped the berry in a stream
And caught a little silver trout.

W.B. Yeats was enchanted by this place and mentions it in his poem 'The Song of the Wandering Aengus'.

Fresh water cray fish

Hazelwood was the seat of the Wynne family, who owned most of the land along the shores of Lough Gill and planted most of the trees that surround Hazelwood, which are less than 250 years old. They made islets on the lake and river; built a shell house, a moss house, a rock house and a windmill that pumped water up to their house. They also planted trees that were not native to Ireland, including hornbeam, cherry, laurel, and Himalayan honeysuckle.

The house, visible from outside the main entrance to the Saehan Factory at the end of Hazelwood road, was built in 1724 for Owen Wynne and was designed by Richard Cassels, who was also

Half Moon Bay

responsible for Leinster House in Dublin and Powerscourt in Wicklow. The view from the house used to offer a fine view of the lake from the east but this is now blocked, and the house is not visible from any part of the trail through the forest.

The Strawberry Tree

Strawberry tree - Arbutus Unedo The popular name of this tree is derived from its round red fruits which ripen in autumn, but the fruits are not as palatable as the name suggests. In fact, the species name of unedo comes from the two Latin words 'un edo', 'I eat one (only)'. It occurs in western France, and on the Mediterranean coast; but, whereas in Ireland it grows to tree size, in Europe it develops only into a shrub. Though able to withstand the sea winds of the Irish coast, the tree quickly succumbs to cold northerly and easterly winds. It occurs in Ireland around Killarney and a few other parts of county Kerry. Here, around Lough Gill, where it is at its most northern limit anywhere in the world there are 36 known specimens in frost free lakeshore locations. It can be found at Hazelwood at Stop 16 on the nature trail. This tree is extremely rare and is a protected species. Do not pick leaves or damage it in any way.

Walks

The short walks here are perhaps some of the most beautiful in the county. The forest trail is a loop of 2 miles (3 km) with two shorter alternatives available at either Stop 10 on the nature trail or at Stop 14.

A series of wooden sculptures is found along the trail. This was the first permanent sculpture trail in Ireland and was created during a symposium held in August 1985. Thereafter the artist, James McKenna, spent two years working on pieces.

Knapweed

Sunset at Hazelwood

Return to the R286 turning left for Sligo City to complete the tour

Detour:

13 Famine Graveyard

When returning to Sligo from Hazelwood, head straight across at the first crossroads and turn right at the small roundabout on Ash Lane (where the N16 begins) turn right at the church to St John's Hospital.

This is on the site of the old workhouse in Sligo. Here, those who died from the effects of hunger and disease were buried, nameless and without ceremony. The workhouse accommodated over 4,000 inmates in the Autumn of 1848. Between 1841 and 1850 over 31,000 people were admitted to the workhouse. It is recorded that there were 2,530 deaths during this time and these were buried in this plot. On July 27th 1997 a bronze sculpture of a hawthorn tree was unveiled to mark the graves of these unknown famine victims. Entitled 'Faoin Sceach' the sculpture represents the 'lone bush'. During famine times people lay down under these trees to die or were buried there. The tree was seen as a sacred protector for the un-named dead. The gates into the graveyard were also erected during the 150 year Famine Commemoration.

The following is an extract from "Rambles in Ireland" by William Bulfin and was written in 1907. It gives a description of his visit to Lough Gill.

"The surface of the lake is smooth enough to reflect everything - the blue sky and the fleecy clouds and the verdant glory of the trees and ferns and meadows and the royal trappings of the heath, and the browns and the greys of the beetling crags. All these tints mingle with the depths, gilded by the glad sunshine that fondly caresses them all. There are bird songs in the trees, and a rabbit scuttles swiftly across the road. You are alone with nature, and you enjoy it."

The Boar of Benbulben Tour
A Tour of Yeats Country and North County Sligo

This drive takes in much of north County Sligo and covers a large part of the Yeats Country Tour. Benbulben is probably the most distinctive of mountains in Ireland. its sheer cliffs rising to its flat top (526m) is one of the most impressive and memorable sites of County Sligo. It is part of the limestone range of the Darty Mountains and has internationally renowned flora of arctic ferns and flowers. It is said that the mountain is named after Gulban, the son of Niall of the Nine Hostages, an important Gaelic king of the 4th century AD. Hence, Benbulben means the 'Peak of Gulban'.

		Page
1	Rosses Point (Walk)	34
2	Drumcliff	35
3	Lissadell House (Walk)	36
4	Ardtermon Castle	38
5	Raghly Harbour (Walk)	38
6	Knocklane Promontory Fort (Detour) (Walk)	38
7	Ballyconnell	39
8	Streedagh (Walk)	39
9	Grange & St Molaise's Park (Walk)	41
10	Classiebawn & Mullaghmore (Walk)	42
11	Dunduff Lake (Walk)	42
12	Creevykeel Court Tomb	43
13	Gleniff Horseshoe drive	44
14	Glencar Lake & Waterfall, County Leitrim	44

Two Bird Mountain Tour
A Circuit of Lough Gill

Lough Gill itself, in its ring of wooded hills and mountains, is one of the most attractive of Irish lakes. There are many legends associated with the lake and its surroundings contain a considerable number of historical and archaeological sites. There are many pleasant walks and picnic spots to choose from, and many of the locations around the lake have strong associations with the poetry of William Butler Yeats. Much of the tour follows part of the Yeats Country Tour. (See the Sligo City Map for starting point).

		Page
1	**Garavogue River & Doorly Park (Walk)**	22
2	**Carns Forest (Walk)**	22
3	**Tobernalt Holy Well**	23
4	**Dooney Rock (Walk)**	23
5	**Slish Wood (Walk)**	24
6	**Castleore Stone Fort**	25
7	**Killery Straining Thread**	25
8	**Innisfree Island**	26
9	**Dromahair, County Leitrim (Walk)**	26
10	**Parke's Castle, County Leitrim**	28
11	**Deerpark (Detour) (Walk)**	28
12	**Hazelwood (Walk)**	30
13	**Famine Graveyard (Detour)**	32

R291
N15
N16
Sligo Harbour
13
Sligo
R292
R286
Calry
11
Colgagh Lough
Viewing Point
Garavogue River
1
2
N4
12
Church Island
Lough Gill
Viewing Point
3
Beezie's Island
4
Carrowroe
5
Killerry Mountain
Lough Dagee
N4
R284
Lough Lumman
Slieve Daeane
6
Ballygawley Lough
R290
Ballygawley

Bay

N15

10

11 12

Cliffony

N15

Ballintrillick

13

bulben

Truskmore

Kings Mountain

Glencar 14

Drumcliff

2 **N16**

Rathcormack

N15

N16

Sligo

Two Bird Mountain Tour

Keelogyboy Mountain

Leean Mountain

R286

10

R286

Carrigeencor Lough

8

R288

Bonet River

9 Dromahair

7

R287

R287

R289

R287

R290

Ballintogher

Boar of Benbulben Tour

Donegal B...

Inishmurray

Sligo Bay

Coney Island

Airport

Strandhill

Carney

The Boar of Benbulben Tour
A Tour of Yeats Country and North County Sligo

The Boar of Benbulben

The story of the enchanted boar of Benbulben associates the mountain with Fionn McCumhail and Diarmait Ó Duibhne, two legendary Irish figures. Gráinne, a beautiful woman and daughter to the High King, was betrothed to Fionn, the leader of a group of elite warriors known as the Fianna. She fell in love with Diarmait, a member of the Fianna, and forced him to elope with her. Fionn's anger was such that he chased the couple all around Ireland. After many years, peace was made between Fionn and Diarmait and the couple finally settled at Graniamore, a townland near Ballymote, County Sligo.

One night, while at his new home, Diarmait was awakened by the sound of hounds barking in the distance and, against the advice of Gráinne decided to investigate. He came to Benbulben, where Fionn and the Fianna were hunting. Fionn told Diarmait that the wild boar had killed fifty of his men, and at that moment the huge boar appeared near the peak of the mountain. Diarmait plunged his sword into the boar and leapt on its back. The two struggled together but Diarmait had dealt a fatal blow to the boar's head. Before the mighty boar died it turned and thrust its tusk into Diarmait's side, fatally wounding him. As the hero lay dying he beseeched Fionn to use his magical powers of healing to save his life by allowing him to drink water from his hands. Fionn collected water in his palms from a nearby spring and as he returned he remembered the humiliation and frustration the younger man had caused him and let the water slip through his fingers. Fionn felt the cold stares of his men upon him

Diarmait and Gráinne's Cave

and this time he collected the water and brought it safely to the dying man. But he was too late. Before he could take a drink Diarmait breathed his last breath on the side of Benbulben.

Fionn's vengeance was only half realised. According to one version of the story, the leader of the Fianna sent the head of Diarmait to Gráinne who died on seeing it. Friends of Diarmait carried her body to a cave and buried the couple together. This cave is known as Diarmait and Gráinne's Cave and is located in the south western corner of Gleniff Valley (see pg. 44).

Start the tour in Sligo City and proceed north on N4 towards the N15, Donegal Road, and take the first left turn after crossing Hughes Bridge on to the R291 for Rosses Point, a total of 6 miles (9.6 km).

1 Rosses Point

Rosses Point is a quiet unspoiled seaside village in a beautiful setting between the mountains of Benbulben and Knocknarea. The Point was a harbour of inspiration for the Yeats brothers - both the painter and the poet.

Walk

You can park the car at the promenade and walk along a footpath towards the yacht club. The small island off the promenade is Oyster Island with the larger Coney Island behind it (see pg. 45). The footpath is sign-posted from the promenade. Heading towards the pier, the ruined building is Elsinore Lodge, reputedly haunted by its builder, John Black, a notorious smuggler of times past. The last resident was Yeats' cousin Henry Middleton. Both of the brothers stayed at **Elsinore and Moyle Lodge**, near its gate, which was the summer house of the Pollexfen family, grandparents of William and Jack. The footpath leads to Sligo Yacht Club and **Deadman's Point**. The old **Pilot House**, which helped guide ships through the deep water channel that flows past the village and into Sligo Port, still stands along the path . The story of Deadman's Point's name stems from a foreign seaman who died and was buried by his ship's crew, who were in a hurry to catch the tide. They were not sure if he was really dead so they buried him with a loaf of bread.

The Pilot House, Rosses Point

Sunset at Rosses Point

The **Metal Man**, in the middle of the channel, is a gigantic statue of a seaman in 19th century clothing, standing on a stone pedestal, and was erected in 1822. His arm points to where the water is deep enough for ships.

Walks
There are three lengths of safe and beautiful beaches to the north of Rosses Point that make up a series of enjoyable seaside walks.

Return towards Sligo on the R291 but take a left turn after 2.2 miles (3.5 km) towards Cregg Hospital. 1 mile (1.6 km) further turn right at T-junction. After another mile (1.6 km) turn left at T-junction and then first right. This takes one on to the N15 where you turn left and through Rathcormack Village. 1.2 miles (1.9 km) after here there is a car-park on the right hand side for Drumcliff Church and Yeats' Grave.

2 Drumcliff
St Columba (521-597 AD) also called Colmcille, founded the important monastic settlement here in the year 574. For many years it was a well known seat of learning, frequented even by foreigners. The monastery was plundered by Vikings in 807 AD. The remains of the round tower, damaged by lightning in 1396, can still be seen.

At the end of the last century some of the stone from the tower was used in the building of Drumcliff Bridge. An 11th century High Cross is nearby, depicting Adam and Eve, Cain's murder of Abel, Daniel in the Lion's Den and Christ in Glory, The Presentation in the Temple and the Crucifixion can also be made out.

Drumcliff is also the final resting place for the poet, W. B. Yeats, who died in 1939 in Roquebrune, France. His wishes were that "If I die here, bury me up there on the mountain (The Cemetery of Roquebrune) and then after a year or so, dig me up and bring me privately to Sligo". True to his

Drumcliff

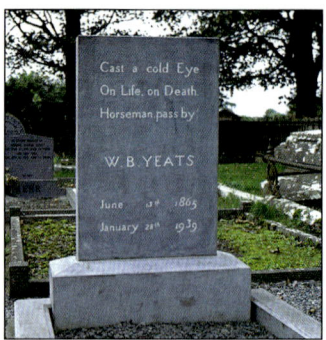

Yeat's Grave at Drumcliff

wishes, his body was interred in the churchyard at Drumcliff in 1948 - where his great-grandfather had been rector. World War II prevented his body being brought to Ireland earlier. The famous epitaph and simple tombstone stem from one of his last poems.

Under bare Ben Bulben's head
In Drumcliff churchyard Yeats is laid.
An ancestor was rector there
Long years ago a church stands near,
By the road an ancient cross,
No marble, no conventional phrase;
On limestone quarried near the spot
By his command these words are cut:
　　Cast a cold eye
　　On life on death.
　　Horseman pass by!

The Church is now a Visitor's Centre focusing on Yeats and Sligo, and aspects of the Drumcliff area.
Opening arrangements - see inside back cover.

Continue on the N15 and take the first left turn shortly after the bridge over the Drumcliff River. After 1.5 miles (2.4 km) you arrive at the village of Carney where you turn left following the signs for Lissadell House, the turn off being on the left 2.4 miles (3.8 km) from Carney.

3 Lissadell House.

The windows of Lissadell House look towards Sligo Bay. William Butler Yeats recalled them in his poem 'In Memory of Eva Gore-Booth and Con Markievicz'.

The Battle of the Books

Cooldrumman is located around the area of Carney Village and was the scene of a battle in 561 AD, instigated by St Colmcille (or Columba). Colmcille had borrowed a famous Psalter from St Finian, and without his permission made a copy of it. Finian brought the complaint to the High King, who made perhaps the earliest copyright order 'To every cow, its calf and every book its copy'. Colmcille and his followers were not convinced by the ruling and took up arms. The armies clashed at Cooldrumman, and over 3,000 men were reputed to have been slain. St Colmcille went to Inishmurray to say his confession to St Molaise and as a penance, he was banished and forced to live a life of exile, converting a number of non-Christians greater than the number killed in Cooldrumman. This he did and established the great monastic settlement of Iona in Scotland.

The light of evening, Lissadell,
Great windows open to the south,
Two sisters in silk kimonos, both
Beautiful, one a gazelle.

The Gore-Booths have lived near Drumcliff since the early 17th century and the present house was built by Sir Robert Gore-Booth in the 1830s. Lissadell holds the legacy of generations of colourful Gore-Booths, including pictures and artefacts collected by Sir Robert on his various tours. His son Sir Henry sailed to the rescue of the Arctic Explorer Leigh Smith, and also kept a large store of food for distribution to his tenants during the Great Famine. In the next generation Sir Josslyn was a keen instigator of the Co-operative movement; Eva was a noted suffragette, and Constance took

Lissadell House

part in the 1916 Easter Rising. She was the first woman elected to the House of Commons at Westminster. It was her husband, Count Casimer Markievicz who created life-size paintings of members of the family and staff, along with the dog, on the walls of the dining room. Lissadell is a fine, but austere, example of Greek-Revival architecture, and as much of the house was last refurbished 100 years ago, visitors can expect a genuine atmosphere of faded grandeur.

Opening Times
1 June-mid September
Mon-Sat   10.30-12.30
          14.00-16.30
Sun   Closed

Information
Contact   Nicholas Prins.
Tel. 071 63150, Fax 071 66906

Walks
The strand at Lissadell can be reached by continuing along the road past the house by car or foot. It is safe to swim and there are many pleasant walks to be enjoyed along the strand or through the demesne of Lissadell. Along the shores here, but particularly to the east of Lissadell at Ballygilgan Strand, a bird sanctuary is the home of 2,000 barnacle geese present from around November to April.

Countess Markievicz

Constance Gore-Booth, later known as Countess Markievicz, was born in 1868. As a young woman and the daughter of a wealthy and aristocratic family, she studied art in Paris where she met and married a Polish count, Casimer Markievicz. After her marriage she returned to Ireland and almost at once her strong patriotic and nationalist views manifested themselves. It was a little ironical that this former lady of society should have figured in the Easter Rebellion of 1916 and be sentenced to death for her efforts in helping to overthrow British rule in Ireland. Her death sentence was later commuted and she was released in 1917. In July of that year she returned to Sligo and was made a Freeman of the Borough at Sligo City Hall. Countess Markievicz successfully contested the General Election of the following year and had the distinction of being the first woman to be elected to the British House of Commons but she never took her seat in that assembly. At the General Elections of 1923 and 1927 she was returned to Dáil Éireann. Her death in July 1927 was widely mourned.

On exiting Lissadell, turn left and stay left, following the signs for Maugherow Church 1.2 miles (1.9 km) from Lissadell, turning right at the next junction. Pass the church and turn left at the next junction. 1.5 miles (2.4 km) from the church brings you to another point of interest - Ardtermon Castle.

4 Ardtermon Castle

This castle was formally owned by the O'Harts and subsequently by the Gore family, ancestors of the Gore-Booths. Sir Francis Gore received the castle from Queen Elizabeth I, and completely remodelled it into a semi-fortified Tudor Mansion in the early 17th century. Two circular towers flank the entrance, and a bawn or defensive wall protects the courtyard. It is fully restored but is privately owned and **not** open to visitors.

Continue on past the castle and straight on to Raghly Harbour, a distance of 1.2 miles (1.9 km). Raghly is also spelt Raugley).

5 Raghly Harbour

Beautifully situated with fine views, this is a small working harbour with nearby strands. It makes a nice place to stop for a picnic. For the most part of the last century this area was constantly affected by blowing sands or tidal floods. Both here, and further on in the tour at Streedagh and Mullaghmore, it was the efforts of Lord Palmerston who arrested the movement of the sands. He introduced large scale planting of bent, a type of coastal grass employed in many golf links.

Walk

There is a short walk from the harbour around the loop of the road and return to the harbour.

Return towards castle but take the first turn left before it, noting the large ringfort on the right after this corner. After 0.8 of a mile (1.3 km) turn left again at a crossroads.

Detour

Take the first left here down a narrow road and park at first corner. (30 minute walk)

6 Knocklane Promontory Fort

The conical shaped hill here is Knocklane, which has spectacular views from its summit. Knocklane promontory fort can be accessed by walking due west along the northern sea side of this peninsula. It could date to the Iron Age (700-450 BC) and is a remarkable example of fortification, with its series of ditches and banks on the east side, and then being surrounded by the sea on the remainder. On the south eastern side of the peninsula is the Derk of Knocklane. The howling sound of both the wind and sea are said to be the haunting cries of the Banshee Bawn, otherwise known as Letitia Gore, wife of Sir Nathaniel of Lissadell. The story about her says that this wild spirited woman forced her coachman at gunpoint to drive her coach along the cliffs here, but both plunged to their deaths in the waters below.

The strand between Knocklane and Raghly, is Yellow Strand, mentioned by Jack. B. Yeats when he said "I have walked Sinbad's Yellow Strand and never shall another take my fancy".

Return to tour

Turn right at the T-junction and left at the crossroads into Ballyconnell.

7 Ballyconnell

There is a dramatic area of coastline here, and at the strands of Ballyconnell and nearby Lackmeeltaun there are rugged rock formations, salt-water pools, and a rich diversity of fossils to be seen. From the strand walk with caution to the rock out-crops to the west, and take in the crashing waves and multitude of fossilised corals in the rocks. The strand at Ballyconnell has an area of bog covered by the sea and at low tide during the summer months locals cut turf as they would at any other bog, only it has to be done before the tide returns!

Return to the crossroads and turn left. Follow road and signposts for Grange turning left and immediate next right 2.4 miles (3.8 km) after the Ballyconnell crossroads. A further 3.6 miles (5.8 km) brings you to a sign post for Streedagh Strand and Streedagh Armada Memorial where you turn left. The memorial is met before the strand.

8 Streedagh

On September 21st 1588 three Spanish Armada ships had become trapped by bad weather off the coast of Sligo. On board one of them was Captain Francisco de Cuellár, who lived to write an incredible account of his adventures. De Cuellár relates that "...we were driven ashore with all three ships upon a beach...within the space of an hour all three ships were broken in pieces, so that there did not escape three hundred men, and more than one thousand were drowned."

The beach in question was Streedagh Strand and the rock nearest the wrecks at the north-eastern end is still called 'Carrig-na-Spanaigh', the Spanish Rock. Many who made it to the beach were killed and robbed by the Irish on the shore. English cavalry arrived later and proceeded to search for and kill any survivors. Many were hung from the rafters of **Staad Abbey** to the south-west of the strand. (Staad Abbey was founded by St Molaise and was a stopover place for the monks of Inishmurray). Some weeks later, Fitzwilliam, the Lord Deputy witnessed 1200-1300 dead bodies on the shore, and commented on the enormous size of the wrecked ships. English divers located the ships in 1985 and recovered a number of items from the wreck. Only during certain tides can parts of the wrecks' timbers be seen. Also at Streedagh there is a dune system based on a shingle ridge, which is of international importance because it supports the plant, insect and bird life associated with dunes. The limestone rocks along the strand are laced with varieties of fossil coral.

Figurehead from a Spanish Galleon wrecked at Streedagh

Walks
It is a stunning place to go for a walk, especially down to the far end of the strand towards 'Carrig-na-Spanaigh'. The walk here and back is 1 hour or more. Park at the beach. Walk to the end, and you have a choice of returning the same way or coming back through the dunes making it more strenuous. There are many lovely grassy paths carpeted with all sorts of wild flowers, and some beautiful picnic spots at the back of the dunes. This walk is affected by the tide. A full tide will make it impossible to walk the full length of the beach. Alternatively walk the dunes or walk along the small beach road, or walk the headland from the first beach.

Inishmurray Island
Inishmurray Island can be seen 6 km off Streedagh Point. It is a 2 km long island - low-lying and bleak. On this small island is a remarkable assemblage of Early Christian remains which give a good idea of what monastic settlements were like.

The monastery was founded by St Molaise probably in the 6th century and was one of the first to be plundered by the Vikings in the 8th century. Within the oval enclosure there is a number of

Inishmurray's monastic remains

Eider Ducks

buildings such as 'Teampall na bFear' (The Men's Church) and 'Teach Molaise' (St Molaise's Church). A wooden statue of the saint which was inside, is now in the National Museum in Dublin (illustrated below) Nearby are 3 altars or 'leachts' with upright cross-engraved slabs, one of which has the famous 'Clocha Breaca' or speckled stones (some decorated or having crosses carved on them). These it is said when turned anti-clockwise can bring harm to one's enemies and are known as cursing stones. There is a large, oval corbel-roofed building known as the Schoolhouse, from its re-use for that purpose by the islanders. Nearby is 'Teach na Teinne' (House of Fire), a medieval building that housed a perpetual fire. There are 50 engraved slabs and pillars in the monastic enclosure and on altars around the island.

In the year 1880 the island had a total of 102 inhabitants, but this had fallen away to 46 by the time of its evacuation in November 1948, when the relative affluence of life off the island drew people away. The island is now a protected and internationally important bird reserve. The bird reserve attracts many species, but is best known for its colony of about 100 breeding pairs of eider duck.

The island can only be accessed by boat in suitable weather conditions.
Boats can be arranged privately through Lomax Boats at Mullaghmore Village (071 66124) or Tommy McCallion at Rosses Point (071 42391). There are excellent books published on Inishmurray by P.Heraughty and J. McGowan.

Return to the Grange Road and turn left, a distance of 2 miles (3.2 km). Turn left at Grange and park opposite the church at St Molaise's Park.

9 Grange and St Molaise Park
An attractive riverside park is located in the centre of Grange Village where there is a replica of the Statue of St Molaise of Inishmurray, found in Teach Molaise on the island.

Walks
Rinroe circular walk is a quiet country back road and the walk lasts approximately 20 minutes. From the car park cross the road, take the road opposite the telephone box down by Lang's pub and the parish hall, continue on. At the first junction after the group of houses take the road around to the left. Follow the road as it is on the map. You will follow a circle which will cross over at the bridge on the river. When you come to the main Streedagh road bear left back to the car-park.
A walk to **Moneygold** takes approximately 1 hour if the complete walk is undertaken. From St. Molaise car-park walk in the direction of Donegal (north) out of the village. Take the first road on the

**St Molaise
(National Museum of Ireland)**

left after the speed signs. When you reach the top of the hill the views are outstanding. Follow the road all the way down to the sea. If the tide is out continue along the rocky shore on the right until you come to a road leading up from the sea (if on reaching the shore the tide is in fully return the same route). Follow this road until you reach the main road where you turn right back towards Grange village.

A walk to **Milk Harbour** lasting 30 minutes. Park at the National School (on right) 2 miles (3.2 km) north of Grange on the N15 Donegal road. Walk back towards Grange village on the right hand side of the road. Continue up the hill on the main road, turn down toward the sea at the Armada Lodge B & B sign. Continue down this road and follow it around to the right to the harbour, which is dotted with fishing vessels. Dernish Island is close by. Continue back up towards the main road by completing the circle.

From Grange head north on the N15 to Cliffoney, a distance of four miles (6.4 km), turn left on to the R279 to Mullaghmore.

10 Classiebawn and Mullaghmore

The prominent building visible for many miles is Classiebawn Castle. It was commenced by the Third Viscount Palmerston, MP, Foreign Secretary and later Prime Minister of Britain (1784-1865), and was intended for his daughter who suffered from tuberculosis in the days when fresh air was a prescribed cure. Palmerston did much to improve the 2,000 acre estate - he built the harbour, both the Catholic and Church of Ireland schools, and gave the parish priest a glebe house to put him on a level with the parson. The Castle was built almost entirely of stone brought by sea from Donegal. Lord Palmerston died in the year 1865 before the Castle was completed and the estate was left to his stepson, The First Lord Mount Temple (William Cowper Temple) who only completed the building in 1874. On the death of The Second Lord Mount Temple in 1939, Classiebawn passed to his eldest daughter, Edwina, and on her death to her husband, Louis, Earl Mountbatten of Burma. After his tragic death the building became privately owned and is not open to the public.

Walks

This area is another splendid place for walking; either along the white sandy beach of Bunduff Strand, with views of Slieve League in Donegal to the north and Benbulben and Benwiskin to the south east, or a long walk around Mullaghmore Head can be done - along the cliffs with only Inishmurray Island between you and America on the west side. The walk around the headland takes just over an hour. You should drive around the headland if you don't feel like the walk.

Continue the tour by heading straight towards the N15.

11 Bunduff Lake

The habitat around Bunduff Lake is salt-water marshland. The lakes here are well known for the whooper swans which arrive here in October from Iceland. Mallard

Classiebawn Castle

Beach at Mullaghmore

and teal are around all winter and occasionally shoveller, scaup and tufted duck come and go.

Walk

Another walk can be undertaken around Bunduff Lough. Park safely at the first lane way on left after passing the second lake. Walk down this lane-way with the lake on your left. Keep an eye out for the various examples of flora and fauna along here. Turn left at the first T-junction and left again at the next T-junction after about 100m. Follow this road with reed beds and the lake on the left, cross the bridge over the stream draining the lake, and proceed to the next T-junction. Turn left and rejoin your car.

At the crossroads with the N15 turn left and almost immediately there is a car-park on the right, sign-posted for Creevykeel.

12 Creevykeel Court Tomb

This is one of the best examples of a court cairn in Ireland. Dating from the Neolithic Period, (New Stone Age - *c* 4000-2500 BC), it consists of a long, trapeze-shaped cairn enclosing an oval court and a burial chamber of two compartments. The court was where ritual rites were performed. This monument was excavated in 1935 by the Harvard University Archaeological Expedition in Ireland. The finds they uncovered, along with cremated human remains, include decorated and undecorated Neolithic pottery, leaf shaped flint arrow heads and hollow scrapers, a chalk ball and polished stone axes - all of which are now preserved in the National Museum in Dublin. The small round structure in the north-west corner of the court was also uncovered - this is attributed to iron smelting activities during the Early Christian Period.

Cliffs of Annacoona

Return to the crossroads and turn left. After 3 miles (4.8 km) you reach the Gleniff Horseshoe Road after passing four minor crossroads, the 2nd last of which takes you into Ballintrillick village. Here you can obtain information from the Ballintrillick Environmental Group's office - Tel. 071 76721.

13 Gleniff Horseshoe

The Gleniff Horseshoe Road is a circular drive with spectacular views and dramatic, wild mountains. Truskmore Mountain on the east side of the road is Sligo's tallest mountain at 647 m (2113 ft). The tall cliffs on the left, after the road begins to turn back around to the north, are the Cliffs of Annacoona which yield a rich alpine flora, including the rare Cushion Pink, *Silene Acaulis*. Shortly after one can see the Cave of Diarmait and Gráinne high up on the steep slopes with its immense natural arch. The two-storey ruined building beneath the cave was once a National School. The extraordinarily shaped Benwiskin (514 m) comes into view towards the end of the Horseshoe.

At the end of the Horseshoe Road turn left and continue straight for 8 miles (12.9 km) with Benbulben's scarred northern slopes on your left to return to the N15 where you turn left. After 2.3 miles (3.7 km) turn left again, sign-posted for Yeats Tour, Glencar Lake and Waterfall. Follow the road around and turn left at T-junction. Follow this road for 4.6 miles (7.4 km) to T-junction and turn left. It is another mile (1.6 km) until you reach the car-park for Glencar Waterfall.

14 Glencar Lake and Waterfall

As you reach Glencar Lake with the steep cliffs on your left, you will notice a series of waterfalls cascading from the heights. If there has been rain and the wind is blowing from the south west great spumes of water get blown backwards into the air. The waterfall from **Tormore Mountain** is called *Srúth in Aghaidh an Áird* meaning the 'stream against the wind'. The small island on the lake is actually a crannóg (see pg. 88). Glencar Waterfall cascades down from a rocky headland to a deep pool, white with spray. Yeats immortalised the waterfall in his poem "The Stolen Child."

*Where the wandering water gushes
From the hills above Glen-car,
In pools among the rushes that
scarce could bathe a star,*

Return to the car and continue on that road, heading east towards the N16. Turn right towards Sligo on the high road over Glencar (there is a lay-by about 2 miles (3.2 km) after turning - a good spot for a photo). Sligo City is reached after 9 miles (14.5 km).

Glencar waterfall

Queen Maeve's Tour

A tour of Coolera Peninsula, the eastern end of the Ox Mountains and the coast to Aughris Head.

Knocknarea Mountain

Queen Maeve Tour

The focus of this tour is the legendary Queen of Connacht - Maeve. The great mound of stones on top of Knocknarea's flat-topped summit is known as Miosgán Meadhbha or Maeve's Grave. It is visible for many miles and dominates the top of this prominent mountain. For most part of this tour her cairn can be clearly seen.

The warrior queen Maeve is a primary character in the Táin, one of Ireland's most famous legends which concerns Cúchulainn, who defends Ulster against Maeve's attack.

There are many indications that Maeve is in fact a goddess of sovereignty, one of the group of Irish female deities of war, territory and sexuality.

The legend of her death is quite bizarre, as an 11th century text explains that she was killed by a sling shot consisting of a lump of hard cheese, by her nephew!

Commence the drive from Sligo City, taking the R291 west to Strandhill, which leaves Sligo City via the Bus and Rail stations. After 3 miles (4.8 km) there is a turn off to Coney Island signposted on the right. This can be reached only if the tides are in your favour so these must be checked if you want to visit this small but remarkable place. A lay-by, 4 miles (6.4 km) from Sligo City, on the right hand-side of the road provides a good viewing point of the island.

1 Coney Island

The fourteen pillars that lead the 1.5 mile (2.4 km) route across to the island from Cummeen Strand were erected in 1845 and act as markers to assist getting to the island safely. The name Coney Island means 'Island of the Rabbits', due to their abundance there. It is also called Inishmulclohy or Mulclohy's island after a family that lived there in ancient times.

A man called Captain Carey is deemed to be the man responsible for naming New York's Coney Island. Carey worked as a ship's captain on O'Connor's timber boat, the Arethusa. He frequently sailed to New York, and felt that the small island near the city was similar to this one as both were overrun by rabbits, and he baptised the island 'Coney Island'. The island has many associations with St Patrick. An erratic boulder on the island is called St Patrick's Chair - a wishing chair where you are allowed one wish per year.

Proceed along the R292 for 1 mile (1.6 km) and turn right to Strandhill. Park the car at the end of the road at the sea front. (Before the turn there is a restored thatch cottage called Dolly's Cottage that can be visited.)

2 Strandhill
Strandhill is a seaside resort with a combination of unique natural features, and its long stretches of strand are great for walking - but unsafe for bathing.

Walks

From the cannon on the promenade, walk in a northerly direction either along the seashore with the tide out, along the dunes, or at the back of the dunes to bring you to **Killaspugbrone Church,** said to have been founded by St Patrick. A path that crosses the end of the runway of Sligo's Airport brings one to the church. This was also the original site of Strandhill village, which moved to its present location because of the onslaught of sand and sea erosion. The existing structure was built c 1150 to c 1220 AD and is said to have replaced the original church on the same site. The addition of the tower and other alterations occurred in the 15th and 16th centuries. On the occasion of visiting Killaspugbrone, St Patrick is supposed to have tripped and lost a tooth. He gave it to Bishop Bronus, who was in charge of the church, as a sign of friendship. The Fiacal Phadraig, 'Shrine of St Patrick's Tooth' was made to house the relic. Records indicate it was made for Thomas de Birmingham, c1376 AD. It can be viewed today in the National Museum in Dublin.

St Patrick's Tooth Shrine (National Museum of Ireland)

There is also a walk southwards along the beach to the point, and on round to Culleenamore. It is easier when the tide is out. The dunes are a protected area as they contain well-preserved plant and animal species

Strandhill

46

Maeve's Cairn on Knocknarea

found in this type of habitat. The orchid pictured opposite is a **bee orchid** growing in the dunes here. Wind erosion has been a problem here but efforts are in place to protect the dunes from further erosion. You can cut across the flat gap between the dunes, a short distance from the car-park, to avoid walking around the point. This will also bring you to the beautiful beach at Culleenamore.

Return to the R292 and turn right. After 2 miles (3.2 km) turn left. Sign-posted as a scenic drive. Proceed up hill along this narrow road for half a mile (0.8 km) to a lay-by with a fine view over Ballysadare Bay. A further half mile (0.8 km) brings one to a left turn, sign-posted for Knocknarea.

3 Knocknarea

This is a very rewarding climb, with spectacular views of Slieve League and Donegal to the north, the Ox Mountains, and on a fine day Croagh Patrick south of west, and Lough Gill to the east. The walk is 2.5 miles (4 km) long. Take the path from the car-park, the walk gets steeper at the stile and continue

Meadow pipit

to the cairn, returning the same route.

On the summit of Knocknarea Mountain is the huge flat-topped cairn called 'Miosgán Meadhbha' (Maeve's Cairn), 55m in diameter and 10m high. It has not been excavated but probably covers a passage tomb, dating to c3000 BC. A number of kerbstones are visible. Within 5m of the cairn lie two large stones, which have been interpreted as North and South markers. About 400m to the north-east there are the foundations of 5 circular and oval hut sites. Excavations on three of them uncovered hundreds of flint and chert scrapers and arrowheads, a polished stone axe and some pottery, which have been dated to about 3300-2700 BC.

Return to road and turn left to crossroads where you turn right to Ransboro Church, 1.5 miles (2.4 km) from car-park at Knocknarea. Turn left at the crossroads at the church for 1 mile (1.6 km) and just past the Riding Centre (on left) is Carrowmore Visitor Centre car-park on the right.

4 Carrowmore Megalithic Cemetery

This is the largest megalithic cemetery in Ireland and amongst the oldest and most important in Europe. The monuments form an oval shaped cluster around a centrally placed cairn covered monument, 'Listoghill' (Tomb 51). Swedish archaeological teams, led by Burenhult, have been working here since 1977 and have come up with very early construction dates for some of the excavated tombs (4840-4370 BC). The excavations uncover new evidence and new discoveries each season of excavation. The tombs could have been signs of prestige in a stratified community or a sacred area in the centre of a tribal territory - interpretation is varied. All of the tombs have been used for secondary burial a long time after the initial construction, both during the Late Neolithic and the Bronze and Iron Ages. Tomb 7, is a good example of one of the tombs. It consists of a central polygonal chamber surrounded by a boulder circle of 31 boulders. It was dated to 4200 BC, and finds include a large quantity of cremated human bones, together with fragments of antler pins and a stone ball. Quantities of unopened seashells were also found. In a secondary cremation, a flint arrowhead was found dating to 2500 BC, showing the tomb was reused in later periods.

Opening arrangements
March - Sept
Daily   9.30-18.30
Tel.   071 61534

Turn right out of the car-park and take the immediate right. Continue to T-junction, turn left to next T-junction and go left again on to the R292. This is 2 miles (3.2 km) from Carrowmore. This brings one out to another T-junction where you turn right and right again at railway bridge heading for Ballysadare, 1.1 miles (1.7 km) from here.

5 Ballysadare (Baile Easa Dara)

Ballysadare takes its name from the rapids on the Ballysadare River which flows into the sea here and means the 'Town of Dara's Cataract'. It is well known for its fishing. Yeats spent much of his childhood at Avena House in Ballysadare with his granduncle William Middleton, which he described as the most

Carrowmore

Ballysadare Falls

gentle place in the whole of County Sligo. Many say that it was about Ballysadare Yeats wrote one of his better known poems, 'Down by the Sally Gardens'.

Down by the sally gardens my love and I did meet;
She passed the sally gardens with little snow-white feet.
She bid me take life easy, as the leaves grow on the tree;
But I was young and foolish, with her would not agree.

Cross the bridge and turn right on to the Ballina Road - N59. Take the second road on the right (the first being by the shops on the corner). Keep straight down this road which turns into a dirt track as far as the graveyard and church.

6 St Fechin's Church

This is a 7th century church called 'Teampall Mor Fechin'. The present structure, on the older foundation of St Fechin, are of 13th century origin incorporating 12th century features. The church appears to have being repaired, altered, or rebuilt at various periods of time. The door has an arch of heads covered by a hood moulding and there may have been a tympanum. The capitals have rather worn representations of imaginary beasts. It is said that the eleven heads represent the Apostles with Judas excluded. Annals tell us that St Fechin was also abbot at Cong in Mayo and at Fore in Westmeath. He died of Yellow Plague in 664 AD.

Return to the N59 and turn right. After 1 mile (1.6 km) turn right at the church. After 1.5 miles (2.4 km) the road bends left and park

St Fechin's

Lisduff

here to enjoy the panorama. An interpretative information board shows you the various bird and plant species that occur at the naturally diverse salt marsh of Lisduff. Continue on this road to the N59 and turn right. After 0.2 miles (0.3 km) take the first left for Coolaney and Glen Wood. There is a car-park at Glen Wood on the right after 1 mile (1.6 km).

7 Glen Wood

Glen Wood has a pleasant forest walk 1.2 km (0.75 miles) long, and a shaded picnic area. Various tree, plant, bird and animal species can be seen here. Doomore Mountain is above and to the west of the wood, and means 'The Large Mound', referring to the large cairn on the summit. Preserved in Glen Wood are the remains of an upland farm settlement including a field clearance system dating back to the middle 1800's.

A few hundred metres on the right hand side of the road after the wood is a rock known as the **Hungry Rock**. It is said to have got its name from the number of people who died on the road during the famine of the 1840's. According to folklore whoever throws a stone at this rock will never know hunger on his journey.

The Hawk's Well and the correct name for the Ox Mountains.

To the left of the road is a prominent rock outcrop known as the Hawk's Rock (pictured below). Just after this is another rocky hill called Tullaghan Hill near to which is the Hawk's Well. The Hawk's Well, or Tubber Tullaghan, is named in ancient manuscripts as one of the wonders of Ireland because the water apparently is bitter some times, i.e. salty, and sweet at others, i.e. fresh spring water. It is located at Tullaghan Hill on the left hand side of the road and is somewhat difficult to access.

One of many legends concerning the well says that Gamh, a servant of Eremon, one of Ireland's first mythical invaders, was beheaded here at Tullaghan. His head was thrown

The Hawk's Rock

The Hawk's Well

into the well making it enchanted and causing it to contain salt water at one time and fresh water at others. His name was applied to the mountains here - Sliabh Gamh. The word Gamh in the Gaelic language sounds like 'damh' when pronounced. 'Damh' means 'Ox' and it was this incorrect word that gave the mountains their English name.

The people of the district came here to celebrate the great festival of Lughnasa on the last Sunday of July. It is said several cures were effected there. William Butler Yeats wrote about the well in his play "At the Hawk's Well" in 1917.

Continue on for 1.5 miles (2.4 km), crossing the bridge and turning right into Coolaney. Park the car on right hand side of road immediately after crossing the bridge.

8 Coolaney

This is a picturesque village situated beside the Owenbeg River where there is a lovely all-ability river walk which takes you to the top of the village past the old corn mill. The walk starts where you parked your car and comes out at the far end of the village. The corn mill you pass was a thriving business since the 17th century. A new corn mill was built in 1838 and the ruins can be seen today. The small tributary of the Owenbree was used to drive the mill. A saw mill was added to it earlier this century and during World War II it was used to manufacture wooden clogs. The mill closed in the 1940's. Just beyond the bridge you crossed coming into the village is Coolaney Old Bridge, built in the 17th century, which now has trees growing on top of it.

Go through the village and bear right towards Rockfield and Carrowneden, passing the Catholic Church (on right) and the School (on left). A crossroads is met after 4.5 miles (7.2 km). Take the right for scenic drive and <u>*Ladies' Brae.*</u> *After 1.5 miles (2.4 km) there is a picnic area and parking area next to the Owenboy River and forest. (Well worth stopping at and relaxing for a while). A further 3.5 miles (5.6 km) and beginning to descend is another picnic area on the left with a stunning view to the north and along the coast. Queen Maeve's cairn is clearly visible.*

At the next T-junction turn right, and pass Holy Hill Hermitage on the right. This was formerly a Sisters of Mercy Convent and is now the home of Carmelite Hermits. Continue to the next T-junction where you turn left to rejoin the N59 Ballina Road - a distance of 3.5 miles (5.6 km) from the lay-by. Pass Skreen Roman Catholic Church and after 0.8 miles (1.3 km) turn left for Skreen Church of Ireland.

Ladies Brae

9 Skreen

On the right hand side of the road you will notice a pillar. This is above a holy well called Adamnan's Well. On the monument there is a Latin inscription, which, when translated means "Eugene MacDonnell, Vicar of this district, had me erected 1591".

St. Adamnan was the biographer to St Colmcille and died in 704 AD. He founded the church of Skreen in the 7th century. The present ruined church dates to the 14th century. Skreen's name comes from the Latin work "Scrinium", a shrine, because in the church were the bones of Adamnan, and various relics collected by him.

In the graveyard of the Church of Ireland church are 23 box tombs, most of which are in good condition.

Pillar at Skreen

They are the work of a well-known local family of stone masons called the Diamond family, and they span the period 1774-1886. The so-called Black Monument is considered a monument of National importance. Andrew Black erected it over a vault in 1825 to the memory of his father, Alexander, who died in 1810. The north side shows a ploughman, dressed in a top hat and tails, guiding a plough drawn by two horses. The clothing depicted may signify that the ploughman won the clothes at an agricultural show. Surrounding this is a bundle of corn and several minutely carved farming implements.

Cherub Head in Skreen Graveyard

Guillemot

10 Aughris Head

Walk from the Beach Bar turning right down to the Pier. There is a short trail left of the pier going on to the cliffs and it provides a viewing point for many species of sea birds - sea gulls, shags and curlews, storm petrels, guillemots, kittiwakes and fulmars. Seals and dolphins can be also spotted from the cliffs. A walk along the beach can also be enjoyed.

Across the road from the church is the birth place of Sir George Gabriel Stokes (1819-1903) who became a famous scientist and mathematician. He was born in the rectory which preceded the present building. He dedicated his life to the study of mathematics and the causes of natural phenomena in Cambridge University, England.

Continue along this road, which comes back out on to the N59 after 0.5 miles (0.8 km). Turn left and then first right after approximately 300m. After 1.2 miles (1.9 km) at a T-junction turn left and take the second right turn for the Beach Bar at Aughris. Turn right before the pier and park at the Beach Bar.

Shag

Return to the T-junction you turned down for Aughris and turn left. Four miles (6.4 km) from Aughris turn left and cross the Ardnaglass River. And take the next left for Dunmoran Strand, a beautiful quiet stretch of golden sand. Return to the bridge you crossed and turn left to rejoin the tour. Note: If you don't wish to visit Dunmoran Strand continue straight, (not taking the left and crossing the bridge), which brings you back on to the N59. Turn left, passing through Beltra Woods and return to Ballysadare - a distance of 12 miles (19.3 km).

At Ballysadare turn right, passing the Thatch Pub on right. A bend at the railway bridge is close to the site of the Battle of Carricknagat.

Kittiwake

A little further on, on the left, is a statue of the hero of this battle - Bartholomew Teeling.

11 The Battle of Carricknagat
This life-sized figure of Teeling, erected in 1898 overlooks the battlefield of Carricknagat. In 1798 a French invasion force under General Humbert landed in Killala Bay to assist in an Irish rebellion.

Their advance was halted here at Carricknagat by an English force which had installed cannon on Union Rock - the rocky outcrop just to the west of here. Captain Bartholomew Teeling was an Irishman serving in the French Army and Humbert's Chief Aide de Camp. After an hour of fighting the French force could not advance because of the cannon emplacement. Teeling galloped from the French ranks, rode swiftly up the hill with his pistol in his hand, shot the cannon's marksman and captured the cannon. The English fled back to Sligo, leaving 60 dead and 100 prisoners taken. The French later surrendered at Ballinamuck in County Longford. The French prisoners were allowed back to France but the Irish who fought with them faced hanging. Teeling was refused prisoner-of-war treatment and was hanged outside Arbour Hill Prison in Dublin, still wearing his French uniform and a tri-colour in his hat.

In the early 1920's the English Black-and-Tans aroused local anger when a passing patrol shot off Teeling's upraised right hand.

Continue into Collooney and turn left taking the bridge over the River Owenmore

12 Collooney
The Church of the Assumption with its elegant spire was built in 1847 from the design of Sir John Benson, a native of Collooney. The Protestant Church was first erected in 1720, but in 1837 it was enlarged and improved from designs by Sir John Benson.

Turn left again and proceed straight across the roundabout on the N4 Collooney/Ballysadare by-pass, taking the exit for Ballintogher on the R290. Within a short distance is the entrance to Markree Castle, which now functions as a hotel.

Grey Wagtail on River Owenmore

The old gatehouse to Markree located just off the N4 road to Dublin

13 Markree Castle

This castle has been home to the Cooper family since Cromwell's time. A 17th century house built by Cornet Cooper was refaced in 1803 in a castle style. In 1832 Edward Cooper, an amateur astronomer, founded an observatory there. The Markree telescope went to Hong Kong in 1932.

Fushia growing near Markree

Continue on the R290 for 2 miles (3.2 km) to Ballygawley Village and turn left on to the Sligo/Cavan Road, the R284. After 1 mile (1.6 km) park your car at the lay-by on the left at Ballygawley Lough. This is set amidst Union Wood and has a short lakeside walk. The numbered posts belong to a study being carried out there.

14 Ballygawley Lough

The small car-park gives easy access to parts of the shore and to a picnic site.

The local rock type is unique, and is part of the Ox Mountains inlier (a metamorphic complex, formed between 1700 and 700 million years ago). Formerly an Irish oak woodland, and part of the Markree estate, it is in a very dynamic phase of regeneration and is now being managed, to allow favoured species, such as Sessile oak saplings, to grow unhindered. There is a diverse flora of common and uncommon species.

Otters are seen occasionally, as well as pine marten, badger, fallow and roe deer, red squirrel, fox and wood mice.

Many birds have also been recorded, including goldcrests, long-tailed tits and treecreepers,

Otter

Bluebells and wild garlic

sparrow hawks, peregrine falcon, an extended family of jays, ravens and various finches, tits, thrushes and warblers. There are also various waterfowl present, such as resident mute swans, whooper swans, coot, water rail, little grebe, teal, goldeneye, wigeon, herons and cormorant.

A large, rarely encountered, parasitic fly, the Gross Tachinid, which parasitises caterpillars, has been observed feeding on wild Angelica nectar.

Butterflies include the striking Silver-washed Fritillary and Green Hairstreak. Some of the moths include the white Plume moth, the Elephant Hawk-moth, Hummingbird Hawk-moth and Cinnabar moth.

Walks

There are many trails and forest paths to choose from. There is a circular walk - over an hour - that can be done. Walking back towards Ballygawley Village, 100m south of the carpark and turning left at the edge of the wood proceed down a forest path marked by the yellow walking man of the way-marked Sligo Way. Take the first forest path to the left. Follow this for 1.5 km (0.9 miles) keeping left and it brings you to a small lodge and on to the R284. Cross the road through the gate and continue on this forest road for 2 km (1.24 miles), again keeping left. This forest road meets the Sligo Way where two tracks meet. Turn left and follow the yellow walking man back to the main road tuning left on reaching it and back to your car. (One can visit Union Rock by turning right when meeting the Sligo Way and taking the second trail on the right which ascends the hill where there is a fine panoramic view of the Bricklieves and Moytirra to the south and the Dartry mountains to the north).

Return to the car and continue straight along the R284. Turn left at T-junction at Carrowroe after 2 miles (3.2 km) and then turn right for round-about and N4 back to Sligo City

Knocknarea

The Labby Tour
A drive around the Lough Arrow region

The Lough Arrow area of County Sligo is an unspoilt region of outstanding beauty, and is rich in archaeological remains. The tour takes in a circuit of the lake and its hinterland. It also goes to Lough Key and Boyle in County Roscommon, returning via the Curlew mountains. History, archaeology, spectacular scenery, geology, flora and fauna, myth and legend are in abundance in this region. Lough Arrow is a famous trout lake and widely known among anglers, particularly for its mayfly season.

		Page
1	Carrowkeel Megalithic Complex (Walk)	58
2	Riverstown (Detour)	59
3	Castlebaldwin Manor House	60
4	Heapstown Cairn	60
5	Ballindoon Priory	60
6	The Labby Rock (Walk)	61
7	Moytirra (Walk)	62
8	Lough Nasool	62
9	Carrownagilty Bog and Carran Hill (Walk)	63
10	Kilronan & Keadue (Detour)	64
11	Kilmactranny (Short Detour)	65
12	Ambrose O'Higgins' Garden	65
13	Boyle Abbey & King House, Co. Roscommon	66
14	Lough Key (Detour) (Walk)	67
15	The Battle of the Curlews	67
16	Ballinafad Castle	68

Queen Maeve's Tour

A tour of Coolera Peninsula, the eastern end of the Ox mountains and the coast to Aughris head

This tour covers a varied coastal and mountainous route west of Sligo City. From the surf at Strandhill to the summit of Knocknarea Mountain; from Ladies Brae in the Ox Mountains to the sea cliffs of Aughris Head. This drive takes in many interesting and highly scenic areas.

		Page
1	Coney Island	45
2	Strandhill (Walk)	46
3	Knocknarea Mountain (Walk)	47
4	Carrowmore Megalithic Cemetery	48
5	Ballysadare	48
6	St Fechin's Church	49
7	Glen Wood (Walk)	50
8	Coolaney (Walk)	51
9	Skreen	52
10	Aughris Head (Walk)	53
11	The Battle of Carricknagat	54
12	Collooney	54
13	Markree Castle	55
14	Ballygawley Lough (Walk)	55

Queen Maeve Tour

Sligo Bay

Coney Island

Aughris Head

10

Dunmoran Strand

Standhill

2

Skreen

N59

Bally

9

Beltra

Lough Aghree

Ladies Brae

Slieve Gamh or the Ox Mountains

Picnic Area

Owenbeg River

Coolaney

Lough Allen
Carran Hill
Seltannsaggart or Corrie Mountain
R280
Arigna River
Goovagh
Kilronan Mountain
Ballyfarnon
Arigna
1
Lough Skean
Lough Meelagh
10
R285
Keadue
River Shannon
River Feorish
R285
Canal
R284
Leitrim Village
14
Oakport Lake
R285
River Shannon
Lough Eidin
N4

Drumcliff Bay
N16
N15
Rosses Point
1
R291
Sligo Harbour
Viewing Point
Sligo
R292
Knocknarea
3
Lough Gill
4
R292
adare
ay
R287
N4
R284
6
5
Lisduff
Ballysadare
14
Ballygawley Lough
N59
7
11
Collooney
12
Ballygawley
R290
13
N17
8
N4
N17
Owenmore River
River Unshin

The Labby Tour

The Labby Tour
A drive around the Lough Arrow Region.

The Labby Rock

The Labby Tour

The Labby Rock is Ireland's second biggest portal tomb, with a 60 ton capstone built during the Neolithic Period (*c* 4,000-2,500 BC). It is called Labby after the Irish word for bed - *leaba* - as this was one of the places where Diarmait and Gráinne slept while fleeing the wrath of Fionn MacCumhaill after the couple eloped together when Grainne was promised in marriage to Fionn. Local folklore says it is the burial place of Nuada of the Silver Arm, king of the Tuatha de Danann who was killed at the Battle of Moytirra by Balor of the Evil Eye, leader of the Fomorians. It is interesting geologically as the rock is of magnesium limestone which has eroded somewhat from the action of rain. It most likely was one of the many glacial erratics found in the area, dropped by the ice sheets during the Ice Age. Over the years soil and seeds combined to produce a clump of heather, bilberry and other plants on top of the stone and form a microcosm of flora and fauna. Discoloration on the rock is from natural chemical action and lichen growth. Myth, folklore, archaeology, geology, flora and fauna are associated with the Labby Rock - all of these things combined symbolise what this region of Sligo has to offer.

Sections of the Arigna Miner's Way and Historical Trail go through this tour. This is a 143 km way-marked national walking route and sections of it can be walked if you wish.

Commence the tour at Castlebaldwin on the N4, 16 miles (25.7 km) south of Sligo City and 10 miles (16 km) north of Boyle. Tourist Information is available at the Arrow Community Enterprise offices here (Tel. 071 65765)

From the village, head west, following the signs for Carrowkeel Passage Tombs, taking the first left just outside the village. The narrow road climbs

Carrowkeel

up into the Bricklieve Mountains. Turn left at the sign for the Donkey Sanctuary, and take the first right. Go through the gate, remembering to close it behind you. At the first bend there is a small car-parking space and a 30 minute walk will bring you up to the cairns. You can drive up but the road is unpaved and very narrow. Another small car-parking area is reached and the main set of cairns are up the hill to the south. Distance from Castlebaldwin is 4 miles (6.4 km) to top car-park.

1 Carrowkeel

There are 14 cairns located at different prominent positions on the hilltops with a further group of 6 cairns extending west towards Keshcorran Mountain, which is also capped with a large cairn. There are magnificent views of the surrounding countryside, principally to the north and west, and many of the hill and mountain tops visible from here are capped with cairns. Slieve League in Donegal can be made out to the north, with Benbulben, Knocknarea, and the Ox Mountains also clearly visible. On a clear day, the pyramid shaped mountain of Croagh Patrick can be seen on the western horizon.

The main group of cairns was examined in 1911 when 14 cairns were excavated. They were given letters to differentiate them and they portray several variations of the Irish Passage Tomb type with Cairns G and K having classic cruciform shaped chambers with intact dry-stone corbelled roofs. Large amounts of cremated human remains were found, along with beads, pins, pendants and Carrowkeel Ware pottery - the name given to a style of pottery common in most passage tombs. Bronze Age artefacts were also found. There is no evidence of megalithic artwork. Cairn E is the most unusual of the Carrowkeel monuments as it combines a passage tomb built into the northern end of a long cairn with a blind court at the south end. By walking west of the main group of cairns (G, H, K, L) towards Lough Arrow there are c80 hut sites varying from 7 to 15m in diameter located on the Doonavera plateau. The huts are undated, but some consider it to be the village of those who built the monuments at Carrowkeel. The huts' circular foundations can be made out on the exposed limestone paving on the plateau. Ravens and birds of prey are frequently seen in this valley.

The **Rest Home for Donkeys,** where a number of retired donkeys are cared for, can also be visited. This is located on the approach to Carrowkeel.

Cairns G and K

Note: The Arigna Miner's Way and Historical Trail goes near the cairns, but not to them. Do not follow the way marked signs if you wish to visit the cairns.

Return the way you came from Carrowkeel to Castlebaldwin. Here you have the option of detouring to Riverstown by turning left or to stay on the tour by going straight across.

DETOUR

Return to Castlebaldwin from Carrowkeel and turn left, and travel north along the N4 for 5 miles (8 km). Turn right at Drumfin for Riverstown. After two miles (3.2 km) you pass the entrance to Coopershill and a further mile (1.6 km) brings you to Riverstown Village.

Just beyond Drumfin crossroads on the N4, is the **James Morrison Memorial**. James was born near here in 1893 and emigrated to America in 1915. He died in New York in 1947 and was one of the many influential fiddle players to have come out of Sligo. The James Morrison Traditional Music Festival is celebrated annually in Riverstown on the last week-end in July. **Coopershill House** is a fine example of a Georgian family mansion. It was originally built in 1774. It is now a guest house run by the O'Hara family.

2 Riverstown

Riverstown is a small village whose name in Irish means 'town between two rivers' - the Unshin River and the Douglas River. It is a village that is very proud of its agricultural heritage and has an important Vintage Day every year when old steam-powered farm engines are on show. The community there is creating the County Sligo Agricultural Museum and Rural Heritage Park, (opening in October 1999), where rural life of bygone days will be displayed and interpreted.

After crossing the bridge you come to a T-junction where you turn right. This brings you to Heapstown Cairn (see below) where you rejoin the tour. You will miss visiting Castlebaldwin Manor House (below).

After crossing over the N4 take the road by Castlebaldwin Post Office and turn left at the first T-junction. However if you wish to visit Castlebaldwin Manor house turn right here. Park at the first house on the right after a shed. Walk back 15m and enter field through the gate. Access can be muddy after rain. Return to junction to continue the tour.

Riverstown Agricultural Museum

3 Castlebaldwin Manor House

Castlebaldwin Manor House is visible to the south east from the village. It consists of a small two-storey L-plan house built in the 17th century. The rectangular main block has two high gables with their chimney stacks intact. The square projection on the south side originally contained the timber stairwell. The entrance has a drawbar socket and there was a machicolation above the entrance of which only two stones survive, from which missiles or other repellents were dropped on attackers trying to enter the door. The doorway is at external ground level but above present internal ground level, pointing to the presence of a basement or semi-basement. Local folklore says that a Captain Baldwin, a soldier of Cromwell, owned the castle and that while he was away hunting one day, he returned to find his castle burnt down by his servants, who had fled into the Bricklieve Mountains.

The road bends round to the right at a community hall, passes Ballyrush Church, and over the 16th century bridge at the Unshin River which drains Lough Arrow. Following the road for another 2 miles (3.2 km) brings you to Heapstown crossroads, where you turn right, and park your car at the Bow and Arrow Public House. A five minute walk to the north through the crossroads and the stile on the right brings you to Heapstown Cairn.

4 Heapstown Cairn

Heapstown Cairn is 60m in diameter, with a kerb of large limestone slabs around the base. It has not been excavated, but it is thought most likely to be a passage tomb and is considered to be an extension of Carrowkeel. At one time it was much larger, but cartloads of the cairn were removed to build roads and walls during the last century. In the Battle of Moytirra, the cairn is called Carn Ochtriallach. Diancecht was the Tuatha de Danann's physician, and he had created a healing well which cured wounded de Danann warriors. Octriallach was a Fomoire warrior who captured the well and caused it to be blocked with a huge pile of stones. Another legend says it is the burial place of Aillil, brother of Niall of the Nine Hostages and ruler of this part of County Sligo in the 4th century AD.

A mile (1.6 km) further on brings you to another crossroads where you turn right for 0.5 miles (0.8 km) to Ballindoon Dominican Priory. Park car on the right and proceed through the gate.

5 Ballindoon Priory

Ballindoon Priory is beautifully situated on the shores of Lough Arrow and was built in 1507 for the Dominicans by the McDonagh clan who had a castle nearby. This unusual Gothic

Castlebaldwin

Heapstown Cairn

style church has almost identical windows at each end. The most remarkable feature of the church is the central tower and belfry, which also acted as a roof-screen, with a narrow passage and two rooms on the ground floor, and an arrangement of three arches on the first floor. On a slight rise to the north-east of the building is a bullaun stone known as Saint Dominic's Stone. The top of the stone has a cup-shaped hollow, almost always filled with water, and is known for its cure for warts.

In the nave, to the east of the junction of the nave and choir is the tomb of Councillor Terence McDonagh. After the Treaty of Limerick he became the only Catholic barrister during Penal times. He died in 1717. In front of his tombstone is another, belonging to Lame David O'Duigenan, a famous professional scribe, who died in 1696. He lived and worked in this region at Shancough, near Geevagh, and was author of one of the surviving independent versions of the Battle of Moytirra myth.

Turn the car and return to the crossroads where you turn right. Just up the hill you turn left into Cromleach Lodge Hotel and park at the car-park from which there are spectacular views of Lough Arrow and the Bricklieve Mountains. Follow the yellow walking man posts, (part of the Historical Trail way-marked walking route) to the Labby Rock, 10 minutes from the car-park.

6 The Labby Rock

The Labby is an enormous portal tomb or dolmen and is discussed at the introduction of this tour. The monument consists of a well-preserved chamber with the large capstone resting on four supports. Its capstone is a huge limestone block, scarred with fractures caused by weathering. Presumably it was raised in situ, for it is difficult to imagine how it could be transported over any distance. It has not been excavated in modern times, but cremated remains were removed from it in the last century.

Ballindoon

Labby Rock

Walk
You can walk past the Labby if you wish, and as far as the paved road, where you turn right and follow the road to a T-junction where you turn right again and right again at the entrance to Cromleach Lodge to rejoin your car. This takes 45 minutes and there are great views of the lake.

Turn left out of Cromleach Lodge and continue for 2.5 miles (4 km) to Highwood Church and Community centre where you can park. There is a picnic table and lovely view of Lough Arrow 200m back along the road and another picnic table at the back of the church.

7 Moytirra
You are now on the high flat plain of Moytirra, also known as Moytura. Two townlands still bear this name, but the actual area of the Battle of Moytura extends from Kilmactranny as far as Lough Nasool. Moytirra or Maige Tuired means 'plain of pillars' and refers to the fourteen megalithic monuments that exist on or near this limestone upland, along with the lines of glacial erratic boulders such as the massive erect block of limestone called the '**Eglone**' opposite Highwood Community Resource Centre.

Walk
There is an hour's walk that can be made from here. Walk past the church and turn right, following the signs for the Historical Trail. At the bottom of the steep hill turn left and the Black Lake is to your left. The road veers left and now the White Lake is on your right. Follow the road to a T-junction and turn left to bring you back to Highwood.

Turn left after Highwood Church for Geevagh and the first left at the T-junction after 1 mile (1.6 km), and then keep straight on, passing a right turn for Geevagh after 0.25 miles (0.4 km). There are views of Boggadh Bog and the Geevagh valley on the right. Follow this narrow road for 2.7 miles (4.3 km) and Lough Nasool appears on your left just before you reach Lough Bo crossroads.

8 Lough Nasool.
Balor of the Evil Eye was killed by his grandson Lugh Lamhfada, king of the Tuatha de Danann, the gods of Ireland, during the closing stages of the battle of Moytirra. Balor had a single enormous eye whose glance meant instant death to any enemy. Lugh fired a sling shot at Balor driving his eye through his head. The evil eye opened and its destructive power burnt a great hole in the ground

The Eglone

Lough Bo

where it fell. This hole filled with water and hence the formation of Lough Nasool which means 'Lake of the Eye'. Ancient tradition has it that every 100 years the water of the lake vanishes. The lake disappeared in 1833 and again in 1933, then it emptied ahead of schedule in 1965 and again in 1985. The reason for its disappearance has never been fully explained, but some theories argue that complex hydrology and unusual climatic conditions are all contributing factors.

Turn right at the crossroads passing the peaceful lake of Lough Bo, with a picnic area on the east side, and travel for 1.9 miles (3 km) to Conways crossroads where you go straight across the R284). 0.1 miles (160metres) brings you to a T-junction where you turn right. Take the first left turn (reached after 0.4 miles) (0.6 km). Veer left after 0.3 miles (0.5 km) and continue on this narrow winding road for 1 mile (1.6 km) to another T-junction, where you turn right. After 0.8 miles (1.3 km) there is a left turn which brings you to a spectacular viewing point at Carrownagilty along a narrow mountain road. After 0.8 miles (1.3 km) there is a track on the left towards a telephone mast where you can park. A 200 metre walk brings you to a T-junction and a beautiful view. Return to the road you came up from, and turn left to continue the tour.

9 Carrownagilty

This is Carrownagilty bog on the northern slopes of Carran Hill (458m). To the north east and east you can see the mountains of Counties Cavan, Leitrim and Fermanagh. To the north is Lough Gill with Killerry Mountain in front, and Slieve Daene to the west. The Dartry Mountains and Benbulben are behind this, and off in the distance are the sea cliffs of Slieve League in Donegal. North west is Knocknarea with Maeve's cairn on its summit. Going off to the west are the Ox Mountains and in the distance is the peak of Nephin Mountain in Mayo. To the west are the Bricklieve mountains and Keshcorran. On the distant horizon Croagh Patrick's pyramid shaped peak can be seen on a clear day. Turf cutting and commercial forestry are the principle activities in this area and a number of paths can be explored if you wish to go for a walk.

You are now driving through the limestone karst area of Carran Hill. The rocks here were formed during the carboniferous period 300 million years ago. The action of water and ice on the landscape has left great blocks of glacial erratic boulders, exposed limestone outcrops and has created a series of caves and sinkholes. The third deepest cave in Ireland is located here - Pollnagollum - 142m deep.

After 1.6 miles (2.6 km) you meet a T-junction where you turn left.

This mountain road crosses the back of the mountain and drops into the Arigna Valley. You may notice areas of open cast mining as this area was an important coal mining area until the mines closed in 1990. Windmills have replaced the coal as a cleaner method of energy production.

You reach the church of Glenkillamey after 3.9 miles (6.3 km). 1.1 miles (1.7 km) further on take the right turn at the site of an old mine, now being used as a quarry. This is locally known as Staunton's Hill. You soon see a spectacular view of Lough Meelagh to the left, Lough Skean ahead and Lough Arrow to the right. A distance of 3 miles (4.8 km) takes you to a T-junction in Ballyfarnon. <u>Turn left for the detour, turn right to continue tour.</u>

DETOUR

Veering left beyond the village of Ballyfarnon and staying on the R284 for 4 miles (6.4 km) brings you to Kilronan Cemetery

10 Kilronan & Keadue
This is where Turlough O'Carolan (1670 - 1738) the blind song writer and harpist and the last of the Gaelic bards is buried alongside his patrons the McDermott Roes. The O'Carolan Harp Festival takes place annually in nearby Keadue. Opposite the graveyard is Saint Lasair's Holy Well on the shores of Lough Meelagh. Stations or traditional devotions are performed every year on the first Sunday of September. Beside Saint Lasair's well is a large flag-stone supported by 4 stones known as Ronan's Altar and cures for backache are obtained by crawling under it.

By continuing for 1 mile (1.6 km) you reach the village of Keadue.

A replica sweat house is found in the village park. This was a device similar to a Turkish sauna; used to cure various ailments, particularly rheumatism.

Turn the car and return towards Ballyfarnon.
Just after Kilronan Church there is another picnic area to the left, just as the road bends to the right. Located on the shores of Lough Meelagh and with an amenity area for children, this makes a pleasant place for a stroll. A walk through the bluebell woods here can give you a sighting of the ruins of Kilronan Castle, home to the Tennison family, the former landlords of this region.

Continue on through Ballyfarnon and turn left to rejoin the tour.

O'Carolan's Park in Keadue

Crossing the bridge out of Ballyfarnon you take the first right turn on to the Boyle Road. You soon pass the pretty lake of Lough Skean, known for the Whooper swans who winter here. One mile (1.6 km) after the lake is Kilmactranny Creamery and crossroads.

Short Detour

Turn right at the crossroads opposite the National School and up to the Church of Ireland.

Stucaire Stone

11 Kilmactranny

The present church, built in 1815, occupies the earlier site of the church of St Mac a Treanaigh. Many of the ancient tombstones in the cemetery are no longer legible, but it is known that the grave of **Hugh Hyacinth O'Rourke** and the crypt of the Conmees of Heapstown are found there. Hyacinth O'Rourke was a famous duellist who was shot by Philip Perceval. A stone cross on top of a rock in an adjoining field may have been erected in 1686 in memory of Edward McDermott Roe. The rock itself is called the **'Stucaire Stone'** and folklore says it marks the grave of a giant of that name, who was killed during the Battle of Moytirra.

On returning towards the crossroads, the glebe house on the left, with much farm machinery outside, was the home of **Douglas Hyde**, Ireland's first president. He was born at Castlerea in County Roscommon in 1860, and later lived at Kilmactranny until the family moved to Frenchpark in County Roscommon. It is believed that his short stay here deeply influenced him, as he heard from local storytellers many folktales and legends of the area which profoundly affected his future. He helped form the Gaelic League and did much to revive the Irish language. He became president of Ireland in 1938 and died in 1949 aged 89 years.

Continue west towards Boyle and take the first right turn 400m from the crossroads at Kilmactranny. Turn right at the T-junction where you reach the shores of Lough Arrow. One mile (1.6 km) later, just past Rock View Hotel is the Ambrose O'Higgins Memorial Garden.

12 Ambrose O'Higgins

Ambrose O'Higgins

Ambrose O'Higgins was born near here in the early 1720's. He joined the Spanish army in Chile in 1758 and quickly advanced through the ranks. By 1787 he had become the Governor and Captain General of Chile where he served until he was made Viceroy of Peru in 1795. His reforms and improvements to society did much to improve Chile, and earned him respect from the poorer classes and natives of the country He died on March 18th 1801, and was buried in the church of San Pedro in Lima, Peru. He never married, but had a son called Bernardo O'Higgins (1778-1842). Bernardo was the leader of the Chilean independence movement and led the army which triumphed over Spanish forces in 1817, thus winning independence for his country. The gardens were opened by the ambassador of Chile in 1995.

Return the way you came, but keep straight along the lakeshore rather that turning left towards Kilmactranny. Two miles (3.2 km) from the gardens you reach a T-junction where you turn right. Continue straight on this road, which rises to a height called the Rock of Doon, where there are magnificent views of Lough Key and the Plains of Boyle. Turn left on to the N4 and after 0.5 miles (0.8 km) turn right on to the N61 for Boyle. On reaching here the Abbey is to the left, while King House is reached by turning right, and Lough Key by continuing straight on.

Boyle Abbey

13 Boyle Abbey & King House
Boyle Abbey was founded by Maurice O'Duffy for the Cistercian Order in 1161 and was closely associated with the great abbey of Mellifont, County Louth. It survived 400 years of successive wars, raiding and plundering. In the nave 14 carved pillars support arches differing architecturally on the north and south sides, as this is a transitional creation, bridging the Romanesque and Gothic periods. The buildings were used during the 17th and 18th centuries as a garrison for English troops stationed at Boyle.

Lough Key

The building is under the care of Dúchas, the Heritage Service

Opening Times
June - Sept
Daily   09.30-18.30.
Tel. 079 62604.
At other times the keys can be obtained from the caretaker:
M. Mitchell, Abbey House, Boyle.
Tel. 079 62385

King House was the 18th century seat of the Kings, later Earls of Kingston, and was built for Sir Henry King MP c1730, on the site of an earlier house which was destroyed by fire. The family moved to Rockingham, now Lough Key Forest Park, at the end of the 18th century and abandoned the house which subsequently served as a military barracks for the Connacht Rangers - a British Army Regiment. King House now contains a series of exhibitions, which explore the history and pageantry of Connacht Kings and Chieftains and traces the history of Boyle and the King family.

Opening Times
Daily   May-Sept 10.00-18.00
Sat/Sun April-Oct 10.00-18.00
Tel 079 63242, Fax 63243

A tourist information office for Ireland West Tourism is located inside the main gate.
(Tel. 079 62145).

DETOUR

Take the R294 out of Boyle heading south east towards the N4 south for Dublin. On reaching the N4 turn right and take the left turn for Lough Key Forest Park, 3 miles (4.8 km) from Boyle.

14 Lough Key Forest Park
This was the demesne and residence of the King family and

Fallow deer in Lough Key Forest Park

comprises some 350 hectares of mixed woodland, the lake of Lough Key and a number of islands. There are various amenities found in the park. On Trinity Island are the ruins of an abbey founded in 1215. Castle Island with the present 19th century castle was the seat of the McDermotts of Moylurg, former chieftains of the surrounding area. There are many walks and places to explore around the park.

Return the way you came to Boyle to rejoin the tour.

From Boyle head north on the N61 going back towards the N4 north for Sligo. A distance of 0.25 miles, just (0.4 km) outside the town, turn left - sign-posted for the Curlew's Drive. (Alternatively one can take the main N4, which avoids the Curlews and passes the Lough Key viewing Point and the sculpture of 'The Chieftain', commemmorating the various battles that took place here.)

15 The Battle of the Curlews.
The name has nothing to do with the bird - it derives from *Corr Shliabh*, meaning 'Rough Mountains'. Part of this drive follows the ancient road called

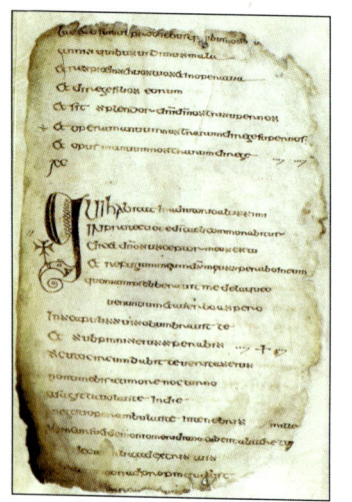

**Page from the 'Cathach'
(Royal Irish Academy)**

'The Red Earl's Road', built by Richard De Burgo in 1300 from Ballymote to Boyle. The strategic importance of these mountains has meant they were the scene of many battles. In 1497 there was a fight between O'Donnell of Tirconnell and McDermott of Moylurg. Not only was the invincible O'Donnell defeated, but he lost the family's treasured *Cathach* - an ancient manuscript said to have been written by St Colmcille and considered the standard of the O'Donnells - its name means 'Battler'. Two years later O'Donnell invaded McDermott's territory and recovered their precious book.

In 1599 Sir Conyers Clifford, the English President of Connacht marched with 2,000 men across this pass into Sligo. He was intercepted by Irish rebels, consisting primarily of O'Rourke and the McDermotts. Red Hugh O'Donnell was camping in the Bricklieve Mountains and was also involved. Clifford's force was defeated and he was killed. His head was sent to Collooney Castle where O'Connor Sligo, who had been fighting for the English, surrendered and joined O'Donnell. Clifford's body was buried by the McDermotts on Trinity Island on Lough Key.

There are incredible views of County Sligo and Lough Arrow as you begin the descent from the mountain pass. Turn right off this road to rejoin the N4 3 miles (4.8 km) after Boyle. Turn left on to the N4. Less than a mile (1 km) brings you to the right turn off the N4 for Ballinafad. The castle is up the left turn at the church and is just after the community hall.

16 Ballinafad Castle

This was built by Captain John St. Barbe between 1590 and 1610. In 1641 the English garrison in the castle resisted assaults by the Burkes and other rebel Irish. It was surrendered to the Irish in 1642. In 1652 it was in the hands of Sir William Taaffe who received it after the Irish surrender to the Cromwellians. The design was modelled on a 13th century plan and stands four storeys high. The main block is dwarfed by four 6m diameter towers. The towers on the north contained a circular timber stair rising the full height of the building.

Return to the village and turn left. This road meets the N4 where you turn right. The wall on your left belongs to Hollybrook Estate. Now closed, this was once the home of the Ffolliot family from 1635 to 1922. Two miles (3.2 km) further brings you back to Castlebaldwin and the end of the tour.

Ballinafad Castle

The Bardic Tour
A Tour through the Ox Mountains and the northern coastline of Tireragh Barony

Enniscrone Castle

The Bardic Tour

This tour commemorates two of Ireland's important bardic families - the MacFirbis Clan and the O'Huiginns. The MacFirbis Clan were the hereditary poets and historiographers to the O'Dowds of Tireragh from the 12th to the 17th centuries. The O'Dowds were one of the leading families in North Connacht from the 9th to the 15th centuries, and their territory originally extended over much of the present County Sligo and into Mayo. Their possessions were later confined to the barony of Tireragh, where they are said to have owned 24 castles. The head of the MacFirbises, who performed a leading role at the inauguration of the O'Dowd chiefs, conducted a school of historical lore at Lacken, near Kilglass, where three celebrated codices were compiled. These were: *The Great Book of Lecan* c1416-18, *The Yellow Book of Lecan* of c1391, and *The Book of the Genealogies of Ireland*, compiled at various places and over many years by An Dubhaltach Óg Mac Firbis (1585-1671), the most famous of the family. Dubhaltach was murdered at Doonflin, near Skreen, at the site of an old inn house by Thomas Crofton, a local squire, and is said to be buried in the old graveyard at Kilglass. The MacFirbises have an exalted position in the annals of Gaelic literature and an undisputed eminence amongst the ranks of Celtic scholars of all ages.

As well as the O'Dowds' territories this tour goes through the lands of the O'Haras. This clan founded a Franciscan Abbey near Lavagh and an Augustinian Friary at Banada. The O'Haras and the O'Connor Sligo families were patrons of the O'Huiginn family of professional poets. Their most famous member was the blind Tadhg Dall O'Huiginn, (1550-1617), the finest bardic poet Sligo ever produced. Tradition says he died after a beating at the hands of six members of the O'Haras of Castle Carragh in 1617 when they allegedly cut out his tongue because of a satire he composed after they abused his hospitality - the last line of which says - I beseech God who shed His blood, since it is but decay for them to be alive - it is scarcely to be called living - that none may slay the troop of six.- the implication being that death was too good for them!

Commence the drive at Enniscrone located on the R297, 8.5 miles (14.3 km) north east of Ballina, County Mayo.

Note: *Enniscrone is also spelt Inishcrone.*

The first point of interest is just after the fire station as you enter this seaside resort on its eastern side. There is a park area with a church and castle to visit.

1 Enniscrone Castle & Valentine's Church

Valentine's Church is named after Rev. Thomas Valentine, who became rector here in 1712 and died in 1765. The church was built around 1712 on an earlier foundation. There is a tombstone set in the wall of the old church,

Enniscrone sunset

The Black Pig

erected to his memory.

Enniscrone Castle, also known as Nolan's castle, is an example of an early 17th century semi-fortified house. It was constructed at a time when the purely defensive nature of castles was being made obsolete by advances in artillery. It is on a site of an earlier castle which was home to the O'Dowd leader. During the rebellion of 1641 the Irish rebels commandeered the castle and placed a garrison there. It was the scene of a skirmish between a local force, led by the O'Dowds, and a convoy of soldiers in 1642. Three years later a Cromwellian army captured it and had possession of it until the end of the war. It then became the property of Sir Francis Gore. The two western towers survive intact but the other two towers have been destroyed since the last century.

Continue into the town and take the third turn to the right to car-park.

You may come across a large sculpted **Black Pig** on Main Street before turning to the car-park. Near Enniscrone is a place called Muckduff, which means 'Black Pig', where there is a cairn of stones. In folklore it is the grave of the Black Pig, a ferocious creature that was chased from Donegal as it went about there devouring children and attacking men and women. It went to sea during the chase and came ashore here, but was overtaken and slain in the present townland of Muckduff.

A bridge across the Bellawaddy River brings you to the 3 mile (4.8 km) long strand of Enniscrone which makes a lovely walk with views of the Mayo mountains and cliffs across the bay of Killala. The tall conical mountain that you can see on this walk is Nephin in County Mayo (806m).

Heading north past the old bath house is **Kilcullen's Seaweed Baths**, established in 1910, where an Edwardian bath of piping hot sea water and seaweed can be had. The old bath house is on the site of one built exclusively for the use of a local landlord, Christopher Orme in 1750. This was extended at the end of the 19th century. The Kilculleens saw the need for extending the premises further and built the second baths at the present location. Originally the water was heated by turf fired furnaces and on a busy Sunday they could use a ton of turf.

A drive or walk away brings one to Cahirmore cliff edge fort, 1 mile (1.6km) from Enniscrone. Head north by the pier and continue straight along a narrow road until it ends at a rocky beach. Park here and walk north, crossing the fence carefully. DO NOT cross the fence at the cliff edge. The land owner is Mr Eamon Mullaney.

2 Cahirmore

This impressive monument is classified as a large D shaped multi-vallate cliff top enclosure, 70m maximum diameter. On the raised area of the interior are the remains of 3 circular hut sites (3-4m in diameter) each defined by a low bank of sod covered stones. The entrance on the south consists of a gap and causeway which extends across the innermost ditch. The fort is connected with the O'Caoimhin family who played an important role as marshal at elections of the O'Dowd chieftains, and hosted the banquet that followed the inauguration.

Leave Enniscrone by continuing on the R297 and after 1.1 miles (1.78 km) take the right fork for the coast road, called the 'Quay Road' for an alternative route to Ballina. After 0.25 miles (0.4 km) a small clump of trees is on the right with a house opposite. Visible among the trees are a number of boulders and an earthen mound. The stones are

Cahirmore

Mermaid Stones

called the Mermaid Stones and are found in Scurmore townland.

3 Mermaid Stones

Mounds like this are dated to the Bronze or early Iron Age and are considered to be burial sites. Immediately adjacent to the mound are six stones, and the following legend relates their story.

"Thady O'Dowd was the chieftain of his clan. One day, while walking along the seashore he saw a beautiful mermaid wearing a cloak, which shimmered like the scales of a fish. Without the cloak the mermaid would remain human and was unable to return to the sea. Thady stole her cloak and asked her to become his bride. She knew he would never relinquish the cloak so she went to live with him. They lived together happily for many years and she bore him seven children. One day his youngest child saw her father hide the cloak and told her mother. While Thady was away at battle she took her children and the cloak to Scurmore. Her children tried to stop her returning to the sea but she could not resist its call and turned six of them into stone taking her youngest with her. It is said that every time an O'Dowd dies the rocks weep."

Continue on for 1.5 miles (2.4 km) and the spire of Killanly Church of Ireland comes into view.

4 Killanly Church

There is a story about the cross being present on the spire - an unusual feature in Church of Ireland churches. Colonel Wingfield lived at nearby Moyview and monitored the progress of the building of the church, completed in 1827. One day he arrived to find the scaffolding was down. But a cross had been erected on the spire which caused the Colonel to become angry. He called for the parson who pleaded ignorance about the presence of the cross. The Colonel could not persuade anyone to climb up to remove the cross - and there it remains. On the shore across the Moy Estuary opposite Killanly are the remains of Rosserk Abbey, County Mayo, said to be the best preserved Franciscan Tertiary Friary in Ireland.

0.5 miles (0.8 km) further on is Castleconor. You cross into County Mayo here. You reach the N59, 3 miles (4.8 km) later, where you turn right.

5 Ballina

Ballina is a busy market town and small seaport, on the estuary of the Moy River where it enters Killala Bay. On the east bank, beside the cathedral are the remains of **Ardnaree** Augustinian Friary, founded by the O'Dowds around 1375. The most famous attraction in Ballina is the **Ridge Pool** where, in the right conditions, one can see hundreds of salmon, and it is extremely popular with anglers.

Proceed straight on, going past the Cathedral and turn left on to the R294 for Bonniconlon, (also spelt Bunnyconnellan) and Tubbercurry. Bonniconlon lies 5.7 miles (9.2 km) away. After this village the road veers left for Tubbercurry and Boyle. It winds up into the Ox Mountains and

Lough Talt

enters County Sligo again at the Windy Gap reaching Lough Talt 4.6 miles (7.4 km) after Bonniconlon. As you enter County Sligo the long wall on the left hand side of the road was built by tenants on the local Taaffe estate in return for food during the famine. There are a number of lay-bys at the Post Office on the left, opposite the public house with two more a little further on.

6 Lough Talt

Lough Talt is in a quiet and beautiful spot. There are two crannogs on the lake (see pg. 88).

Walk

There are a number of walks in this area and it is from here that the Sligo Way commences. One of the walks is a circuit around the lake which is 4 miles (6.4 km) in distance. From the Lough Talt Inn walk towards the south east, Tubbercurry direction on the R294, turn right and follow the path along the lakeshore. The walk moves away from the water's edge on the north western end of the lake and joins a lane which leads back to the R294. Turn right to rejoin your car.

Continue on the R294 for Tubbercurry turning right shortly after Mullaney's Cross, a distance of 2.2 miles (3.5 km) from Lough Talt and heading for Aclare. After 2.4 miles (3.8 km) you reach this small village where you turn left for Banada.

7 Aclare

Aclare is in the Parish of Kilmactigue and situated on the Eignagh River, a tributary of the Moy. To the west of the village is Kilmactigue Catholic Church, built in 1844 and the Church of Ireland Church which is older in date and which closed in 1990. One mile (1.6 km) south of the church are the remains of Belclare castle, an important castle belonging to the O'Hara's dating to the 13th century.

A distance of 2.2 miles (3.5 km) brings you to Toorlestraun Village with its church dating from 1844 and bell dating to 1868. Another 1.2 miles 1.9 km) straight on and you reach Banada. Cross the bridge heading left for Tubbercurry. If you want to explore, there is parking to the right in front of a park area just over this bridge

8 Banada

The park, called the **'Peace Park'**, is next to a handball alley and on the banks of the River Moy. Within the graveyard at Banada are the part remains of **Corpus Christi Priory**, first Irish house of Augustinian friars of Regular Observance. It was founded by Donnchadh O'Hara in 1423. The priory later became the property of the Jones family, the landlords of this area. This Protestant family apparently converted to Catholicism after one of the family raised his arm to strike a priest and his arm became paralysed. The family donated the property to the Irish Sisters of Charity who opened a school there. For want of

Moylough Belt Shrine (National Museum of Ireland)

vocations the sisters left in 1987.

Near Banada, at Coolrecuil, was the residence of the famous blind 16th century poet **Tadhg Dall O'Huiginn** (see pg. 69). Tradition says that after being beaten and mutilated by the O'Haras he sought refuge in Banada Priory where he died from his injuries and was buried in the cemetery there.

Take the road to Tubbercurry. It meets the N17 at a T-junction after 1.2 miles (1.9 km) where you turn left to Tubbercurry - another 1.2 miles (1.9km) away.

9 Tubbercurry

Positioned at the base of the Ox Mountains, this is Sligo's second largest town. It vibrates each July to some of Ireland's best traditional music, as its Summer School of Traditional Music and Dance gets under way (Contact 071 85010 for information). The old fair green in the centre of the town has a sculptured group of musicians and dancing children.

Moylough Belt Shrine

The early 8th century saw the perfection of Irish art. Masterpieces of metal work such as the Tara Brooch, Derrynaflan Paten and Ardagh Chalice were produced during this period. The magnificent illuminated manuscripts such as the Book of Kells were also made during this golden age of Irish art. The important monasteries devoted a great deal of effort to enshrining the relics of their founding saints and other holy men. One such shrine is a unique belt-reliquary that was found at Moylough in

Fair Green in Tubbercurry

County Sligo by a man digging turf in 1945.

The man in question was the late Johnny Towey and it was found in the Moylough bog in the parish of Curry. Mr Towey had dug down about four feet into the turf and found a hard object which he carefully removed and brought home. Many of his neighbours came to see it and the local postman, John Nicholson, persuaded Johnny Towey to notify the National Museum and arrangements were made to have it displayed there. It is now on permanent display in the Treasury Room of the museum.

The shrine still contains the leather strap of a belt - probably a relic of a saint. It consists of four segments hinged together made from tinned bronze, and are highly decorated. The occurrence of many die-stamped silver panels is an rare example of this type of decoration, which also occurs on the Ardagh Chalice. It has a false buckle which, although made in the 8th century, copies the form of Frankish buckles of c600 AD. Despite damage by the acids of the bog, its inlaid studs, stamped silver ornaments, angular panels of enamel and millefiori glass, make it one of the great pieces of the period.

Moylough is located 3.1 miles (5 km) from Tubbercurry. Take the R294 heading east towards Ballymote/Boyle. Take the first right turn at a crossroads as far as the church at Moylough.

Head north on the N17 towards Sligo City. On your right is a forest-covered hill called Muckelty which has a number of important archaeological remains on it,

including an ancient fort and a cairn. Turn left after 4.1 miles (6.5km) at the NCF Creamery, sign-posted for Lavagh. After 1.2 miles (1.9km) you reach Lavagh where you turn right.

Flycatcher

Short Detour

To visit Knocknashee Prehistoric Complex continue straight for 1.2 miles (1.9 km), passing two right turns. Park safely at the first farmhouse on the left (just after passing the second right turn). Enquire at the farmhouse about access up to the mountain from Mr Dermot Scully, who knows much about the area. It is 30 minutes to the summit and the walk is steep towards the top.

10 Knocknashee 'Hill of the Fairies'

This was identified as a fortified hilltop in 1988. It is a massive 700m long and 320m wide. The site is located on a spectacular limestone table-top plateau commanding a widespread view over the north Connacht plain. The area enclosed by two earth and stone ramparts is 53 acres. Two large cairns are situated on the summit and Knocknarea and Carrowkeel/ Keshcorran are clearly visible from them. Spread out along the eastern and relatively sheltered section of the plateau is a group of approximately 30 circular house sites; most are covered by peat. The

Knocknashee Hilltop Fort

scale and commanding location of the site suggest that it was a regional centre at the end of the Bronze Age c1000 BC.

On returning to your car, go back the way you came, and the first turn left brings you to Court Abbey.

11 Court Abbey

This is a 15th century Friary occupied by the Franciscan Tertiaries and established by the O'Haras. The building is dominated by a square central tower nearly 30m high which stands at the junction of the east and west chapels. A unique feature of the west chapel are the wall paintings found on the remaining plaster which can be made out in conditions of high humidity.

Heading back towards Lavagh take the first turn right (before the village) and rejoin the tour.

On leaving Lavagh take the first turn to the left after 0.1 miles (160metres) with Knocknashee Mountain rising on the right. Continue 0.9 miles (1.4 km) to a crossroads where you turn left. Straight across here, however, is Carrowmore School Museum.

12 Carrowmore School Museum

The original school house was built in 1834 and was recently restored by the local community. Within the building is the small teacher's residence and a classroom. Tourist information and refreshments are also available. (Tel. 071 84367). Near to here is the source of the River Moy.

Going back to the crossroads from the school you head west towards the Ox Mountains on this road. Shortly after turning at the crossroads, you pass the old

Carrowmore School Museum

Mass Hill

railway station for Carrowmore, part of the Collooney to Claremorris line which opened in 1895 and closed in 1975. After 2.1 miles (3.4 km) you reach a T-junction where you turn left. You reach Cloonacool Village after 2.4 miles (3.8 km). At 3.8 miles (6.1 km) further on, turn right for Easky Lough. The road starts climbing through a lovely glen after 2.5 miles (4 km). There is a car-park to the left, sign-posted for Mass Hill.

13 Mass Hill

This is the site of a penal mass rock, a place where worshippers went to hear mass during the Penal Laws. Following the Williamite victory over the Jacobites (William of Orange against James II), and the Treaty of Limerick in 1691, the Irish parliament began strengthening all aspects of Protestant ascendancy. A number of laws were passed by the parliament to keep Catholics in a state of subjection. Apart from a number of sporadic persecutions they lost momentum by 1716. However, it did mean that all Catholic church properties were confiscated and all members of the clergy had to go into hiding. A Catholic might have to declare to two Justices of the Peace when he last heard mass and what priest said it or face imprisonment for a year if he failed to answer. Because of the situation masses were held in out-of-the-way places and large rocks were used as make shift altars.

Continue northward towards Easky Lough. After 3.2 miles (5.1 km) you cross a small bridge at the south end of the lake. The Sligo Way comes out here and this can be walked off road for a while, and then return to the car when you wish. A mile (1.6 km) further on there is a car-parking area on the left. A path here brings you along the northern shore of the lake if you wish to walk here.

Easky Lough

Easky Lough

14 Easky Lough

Easky Lough is situated 187m above sea level, and is a wild, barren and remote place, that is breathtakingly beautiful. The landscape here is empty, but the turf-cutters are plentiful during the summer months as most of what you see up here is peat bog.

Before the road descends towards the sea, there is a large ruined house on the right. This is an old hunting lodge used by the local landed gentry. The ptarmigan is no longer found, but there are red grouse and snipe to be seen. A large part of this area to the east of the road is a bird reserve and is a protected habitat for many species.

3.6 miles (5.8 km) further on, you pass a water treatment plant. Continue on for another 3.1 miles (5 km), to a T-junction, where you reach the Ballina-Sligo Road, the N59.

Restored shop in Culkin's Museum

Short Detour
Turn left and take the second left for Culkin's Emigration Museum.

You pass a large building to the right which is the old Dromore West work house. This, and another at Tubbercurry, was built to relieve the huge pressure on the Sligo Workhouse, caused by the huge demand for admission during the Great Famine (see pg. 32).

15 Culkin's Emigration Museum

This small museum relives a poignant era of emigration. The museum, on a site where once stood the gateway to the new worlds in the form of Daniel Culkin's Shipping and Emigration Agency, brings back to life this landmark - which operated from the 19th century right up to the 1930s. There are a number of interesting artefacts and features such as the original shop itself, now restored and housed within the building.

Opening arrangements:
June-Sept
Mon-Sat	10.00-17.00
Sun	13.00-17.00

Rosslee Castle

Contact
Tel.   096 47152
Fax   096 47416

Turn right on to the N59 and 1 mile (1.6 km) further on is the village of Dromore West. Turn left here on to the R297 for Easky and Enniscrone. After 0.7 miles (1.1 km), passing the water tower bear left at the T-junction.

Note: *Enniscrone is also spelt Inishcrone).*

Continue on for 1.5 miles (2.4 km) and park, or slow down at a National School on the right hand side. Just opposite this, on your left, but difficult to see coming from this direction, is Fionn Mac Cumhaill's Split Rock.

16 The Split Rock
Fionn Mac Cumhaill's Split Rock is an erratic boulder dropped by a glacier during the last ice age. This particular stone was thrown here by the legendary Fionn MacCumhaill. He made a bet that he could throw the rock from the Ox Mountains to the sea. However, the rock fell short of its target, and the furious Fionn ran down to it and struck it with his sword, splitting it in two. It is said that the rock will close on anyone who dares walk through the cleft three times!

Another 1.5 miles (2.4 km) brings you to Easky Village

17 Easky
Easky is well known for its fishing and surfing. The river is well known by fishermen and the name Easky means 'fish'. In the village is the Tourist Information and Surfing Centre. If you park your car here, there is a riverside walk that crosses the bridge and follows the river to the

Surfing at Easky

coast to Roslee Castle and to the main site for surfers. Dating to the 15th century the castle was the former stronghold of the MacDonnells who were Gallowglasses (Scottish mercenary soldiers) in the service of the O'Dowds of Tireragh. King James I granted it to Daniel O'Dowd in 1618. A story tells of the owners having a wire attached from a net in the river to a bell in the kitchen of the castle. As soon as a salmon entered the trap the bell rang and the servants went immediately, fetched the salmon, and prepared it for their master.

Continue on the R297 for Enniscrone reaching Rathlee Village Post Office after 3.1 miles (5 km).

Red shank

A further 2.9 miles (4.6 km) after Rathlee brings one to Kilglass. Nearby, and towards the coast, was the location of **Lacken Castle (alias Lecan)**. The castle was erected in 1560 by the MacFirbis Clan who were the hereditary poets and historiographers to the O'Dowds of Tireragh from the 12th to the 17th centuries. (see pg. 69) Tradition says Dubhaltach (Dudley in English) is buried in the old graveyard at Kilglass.

It is a distance of 6.6 miles (10.6 km) from Rathlee to Enniscrone, where you complete the tour.

**Book of Lecan
(Royal irish Academy)**

The Tour of Corran
Harpist of the Tuatha de Danann
A tour of Ballymote, Gurteen and Lough Gara in South County Sligo

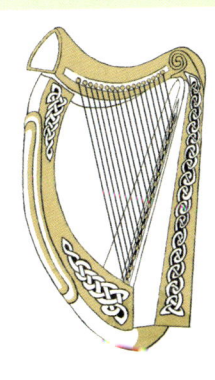

This tour takes in part of south Sligo, extending from Ballymote to Lough Gara to Boyle and back to Ballymote via Keash. Lough Gara, the Curlew Mountains and the western side of the Bricklieve Mountains are also visited. The tour also goes through what is known as Coleman Country - an area around Gurteen where some of Ireland's best traditional musicians were from, including the famous fiddler, Michael Coleman.

		Page
1	**Ballymote (Walk)**	81
2	**Templehouse (Detour)**	83
3	**Achonry Cathedral (Same Detour)**	84
4	**Gurteen & Michael Coleman**	84
5	**Carrowntemple Slabs**	85
6	**Clogher Cashel**	86
7	**St Attracta's Well (Walk)**	86
8	**Lough Gara & Crannógs**	88
9	**Moygara Castle**	89
10	**Viewing Point of Lough Gara**	89
11	**Toomour**	90
12	**Keshcorran Caves (Walk)**	91

The Bardic Tour

A tour through the Ox Mountains and the northern coastline of Tireragh Barony

This route takes in the western end of the Ox Mountains in County Sligo and the coast from Dromore West to Enniscrone. It is a highly scenic drive with a great deal of variation of landscape. From the limestone mountain of Knocknashee with its archaeological remains, to the bleak and wild shores of Lough Easky; and from the miles of golden sand of Enniscrone strand to the traditional music centre of Tubbercurry.

		Page
1	**Enniscrone Castle & Valentine's Church (Walk)**	70
2	**Cahirmore Cliff-edge Fort (Walk)**	71
3	**Mermaid Stones**	72
4	**Killanly Church**	72
5	**Ballina, County Mayo**	72
6	**Lough Talt (Walk)**	73
7	**Aclare**	73
8	**Banada**	73
9	**Tubbercurry**	74
10	**Knocknashee (Short Detour) (Walk)**	75
11	**Court Abbey (Same Detour)**	76
12	**Carrowmore School Museum**	76
13	**Mass Hill**	77
14	**Lough Easky (Walk)**	78
15	**Culkin's Emigration Museum (Short Detour)**	78
16	**The Split Rock**	79
17	**Easky Village**	79

The Bardic Tour

Killala Bay

Easky
R297
17
16

Kilglass
Easky River
2
1
Enniscrone
R298
N59
15
3
R297
4
R314
N59
N59
Ballina
Brusna River
5
Bonniconlon
R294
6
Lo
Ta
N26
River Moy
Slieve Gamh of the Ox Mountains
Kilmactig
Lough Rive
Lough Conn
To Foxfor
Riv
Mo

To Sligo
N4
River Unshin
note
Castlebaldwin
R295
R293
12 Keshcorran
Keash Post Office
Bricklieve Mountains
Lough Arrow
11
Culfadda
Ballinafad
R295
Curlew Mountains
10
N4
R294
Cloonloo
Boyle
R294
9
Boyle River
Lough Gara
8
Lough Gara

Atlantic Ocean

- Dromore West
- Templeboy
- Skreen
- Ardnaglass River
- N59
- To Ballysadare
- Waterworks
- Ladies Bk
- Owenbeg River
- 14 Lough Easky
- 13
- 12
- Knockashee
- 10
- 11
- Lavagh
- Cloonacool
- NCF Creamery
- Muckelty Hill
- River Moy
- N17
- **Tubercurry**
- 9
- R294
- R294
- To Ballymote & Boyle
- 7 Aclare
- Toorlestraun
- Banada
- 8
- Moylough
- N17
- Curry
- To Charlestown

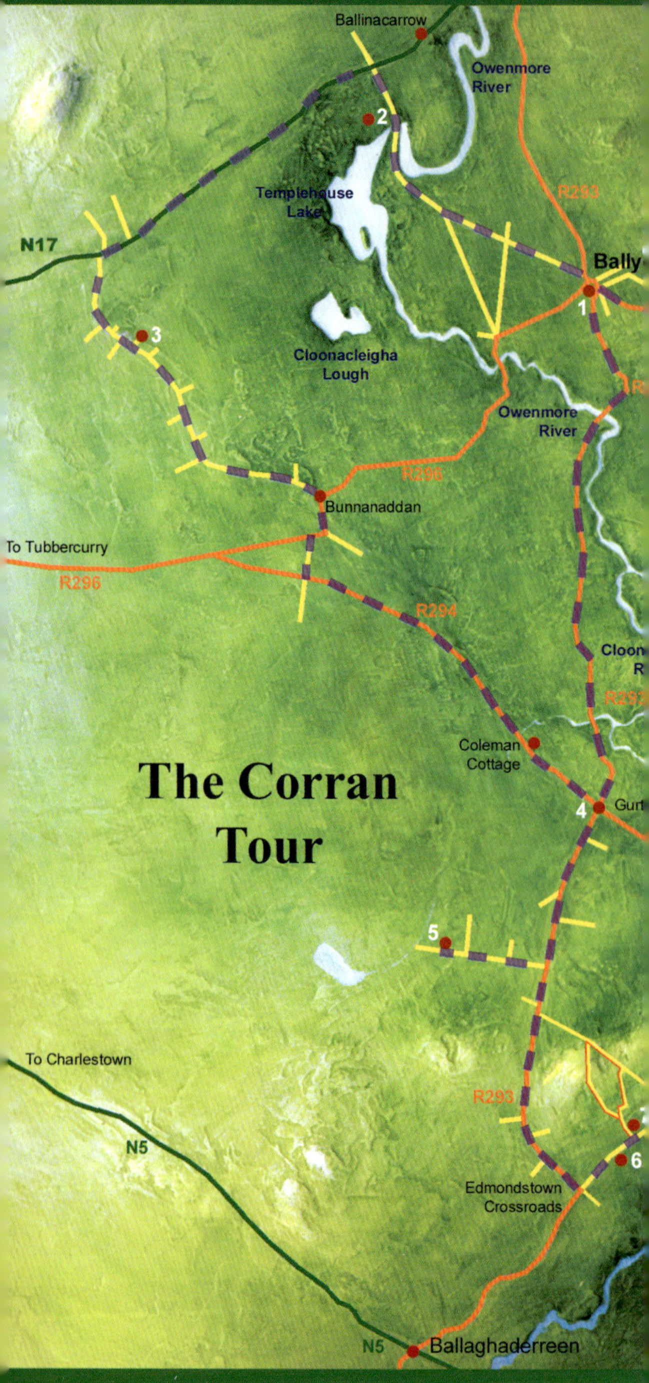

The Corran Tour

- Ballinacarrow
- Owenmore River
- Templehouse Lake
- N17
- Bally
- R293
- Cloonacleigha Lough
- Owenmore River
- Bunnanaddan
- To Tubbercurry
- R296
- R294
- Cloon R
- Coleman Cottage
- Gurt
- To Charlestown
- N5
- R293
- Edmondstown Crossroads
- N5 Ballaghaderreen

Tour of Corran
Harpist of the Tuatha de Danann
A tour of Ballymote, Gurteen and Lough Gara in South County Sligo

The Corran Tour

The tour goes through the Baronies of Corran and Coolavin. The Dindshenchas legends - 'the lore of places' - tell us that the lands of this region were granted to Corran, the harper of the Tuatha de Danann - 'the people of the goddess Danú'. These were a race of divine beings - the gods of Irish mythology, who inhabited Ireland before the arrival of the Gaels (the sons of Mil). The Dindshenchas say that "To Corran of the soft music the Tuatha de Danann gave with great honour, a free territory for his skilful playing, his knowledge and his astrology". Corran is said to have dwelt in the caves of Keshcorran. The mountain of Keshcorran (359m) with its cairn of stones on the summit, is visible from many parts of the tour.

Start the tour at Ballymote

1 Ballymote

Ballymote is a busy thriving town with a large cattle mart. The best way to view Ballymote is by walking through its linear **Heritage Park** and return by walking through the town along O'Connell Street and Lord Edward Street.

The entrance to the Heritage Park is at the north end of the town, next to a petrol station on the R293 road towards the N17 and Sligo City.

The Franciscan Friary

In 1442 Pope Eugene IV issued a Papal License for a Third Order Regular Franciscan House at Ballymote at the request of Cugaragh McDonagh. The medieval structure is rectangular in shape with a

Pope Eugene IV

Ballymote's Train Station

large east window, under which stood the Altar. The west door is surmounted by a stone carving which local tradition identifies as Pope Eugene IV with a Papal Tiara.

The **Church of the Immaculate Conception** was completed in 1864 by George Goldie. The site was donated by Sir Robert Gore-Booth of Lissadell who owned the lands of Ballymote at the time. Securing a solid foundation proved to be difficult and huge bales of wool were used in the foundations.

On December 3rd 1862 the first train steamed into **Ballymote Railway Station.** Apart from being convenient for passengers, the opening of the station helped the town advance towards prosperity.

Drawing of a boat from the Book of Ballymote (Royal Irish Academy)

Ballymote Castle
Richard de Burgo, the "Red Earl" of Ulster, built the remains of this Anglo-Norman castle in AD 1300 and it was the strongest fortress in Connacht.

Later, the O'Connors, the MacDonaghs, O'Connor Sligo, and Sir Richard Bingham owned it. It returned to the MacDonaghs who sold it for £400 and 300 cows to Red Hugh O'Donnell in 1598. It was from here that O'Donnell marched to the disastrous Irish defeat at Kinsale in 1601. In 1690 it was held by one of the O'Connors but he surrendered it to the Williamites and soon afterwards it was abandoned.

The most prominent feature of this impressive fortification is the large gate building - a rectangular structure with projecting half round towers at each side of the entrance. Ballymote Castle is almost square in plan with a three quarter round tower at each angle and a D-shaped tower mid-way along the east and west curtains. In the south wall there is a small gateway - which may have been used as a sallyport.

The famous Codex, **'The Book of Ballymote'** was probably compiled here c1400 AD. This is now in the Royal Irish Academy, Dublin.

Continue to the end of the park, turn left and left again.

Returning back through the town you pass the **Church of Ireland** on the right, built in 1818 and

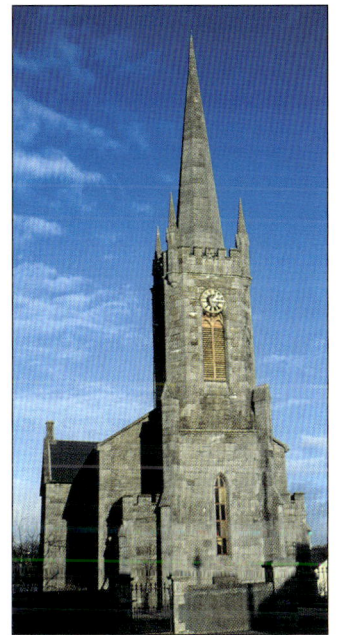

Ballymote Church of ireland

renovated with the help of Sir Robert Gore-Booth in 1848.

Return to your car by turning left on reaching Teeling Street and then right.

OPTIONAL DETOUR

From the R293 on the north side of Ballymote Town and just after the entrance to the Heritage Park turn left on road sign posted for Templehouse. After 2.9 miles (4.9 km) turn right at the T-junction.

2 Templehouse

The woods on either side of the

Gatelodge to Templehouse

Grebe on Templehouse Lake

road belong to the demesne of Templehouse Estate.

0.6 miles (0.96 km) after turning there is a lay-by on the right by the banks of the Owenmore River, a good place for fishing. Just after the lay-by is a bridge over the Owenmore River, which flows from Templehouse Lake.

Templehouse has been home to the Perceval family since the 17th century. Opposite their mansion are the remains of a 13th century castle built by the Knights Templar who were there until their suppression in 1312. It was later owned by the O'Haras. The estate includes the beautiful Templehouse Lake. The house has different periods of construction, but mainly dates from 1863 and contains many original furnishings. **The grounds and house are private and not open to visitors**

Continue for 0.9 miles (1.45 km) until the N17 and turn left towards Tubbercurry. Knocknashee Mountain is clearly visible to the right (see pg. 75). After 4 miles (6.43 km) there is a large creamery (NCF) on the right and

Achonry Cathedral

immediately after this turn left towards Bunnanaddan. After 1.5 miles (2.4 km) on the left hand side there is a sign for Achonry Cathedral.

3 Achonry Cathedral

This is the site of **St Nathy's** church at Achonry. St Finnian of Clonard founded a monastery here in the 6th century and left his disciple St Nathy in charge. The site was of considerable religious importance, and became a diocese in the 12th century. The present small Church of Ireland Cathedral dates to 1823 and is closed at present. This had the distinction of being the smallest cathedral in Ireland.

Continue along this road for 3.2 miles (5.15 km) to Bunnanaddan and turn right on to the R296 towards Tubbercurry. After 0.5 miles (0.8 km) turn right at signpost for Charlestown. After 0.9 miles turn left at the crossroads on to the R294 for Gurteen and Boyle. A further 2.3 miles brings you to the Coleman Cottage (see below). Gurteen village is another 2.7 miles where you rejoin the tour.

If you decide not to do the detour take the R293 for Ballaghdereen and Gurteen at the south end of Ballymote, a distance of 7.5 miles (12 km). The road crosses the Sligo-Dublin railway line and weaves through the Drumlin landscape created over 10,000 years ago by the action of Ice Age glaciers. The road also passes the flood plains of the Owenmore River to the left of the road.

4 Gurteen

This is Coleman Country, a place synonymous with Michael Coleman, one of Ireland's most famous fiddle players. Gurteen and the surrounding areas have produced many talented traditional Irish musicians, including Fred Finn and Peter Horan of Killavil.

On reaching the crossroads at Gurteen you find the Coleman Heritage Centre (Tel. 071 82599), which focuses on the musical traditions of the area with particular reference to Michael Coleman. Music workshops and musical performances are held here throughout the year.

Short detour

A short drive to the birth place of Michael Coleman can be made by turning right at the crossroads and travelling 2.7 miles on the R294. This consists of a reconstruction of the Coleman Homeplace, a forge, a lime kiln and outbuildings, and it gives an insight into life at the turn of the 19th century.

Michael Coleman

Michael Coleman was born in 1891, son of Jamsey and Bessie Coleman, and was the last of ten children. His father was a great flute player and Michael learned music at an early age. His brother Jim, eight years his senior, was an exceptional fiddle player and highly gifted.

Michael went to America in 1914 where he was soon playing at many entertainment centres throughout New York. In early 1921 he made his first records and he went on to record eighty tracks including his greatest pieces: 'The Grey Goose', 'The Green Fields of America', 'The Swallows Tail' and 'Lord McDonald'. His records also became highly popular in Ireland, as did the style of fiddle playing he used.

His brother Jim stayed at home and had he moved away, perhaps he would have achieved even more success than his brother. Michael Coleman died in New York in 1945.

Take the R293 heading south out of Gurteen, towards Ballaghadereen. Pass a public house and then Kilfree Post Office turn right - 2.4 miles (3.86 km) from Gurteen. Signposted 'Carrrentemple Burial Grounds'. Proceed 1.3 miles and the graveyard is on the right.

5 Carrowntemple Slabs

Carrowntemple has an early Christian ecclesiastical enclosure evident from the air, but difficult to see on the ground. The fourteen inscribed slabs at Carrowntemple may represent the work of several different

Human Figure at Carrowntemple

people, artists and stone carvers. Many of the motifs reflect a type of interlacing knotwork common to decorative Irish art between the 8th and 10th century. These beautiful stones became endangered, and for their preservation they were removed in 1992 and these excellent copies in the same type of sandstone replaced them. The original human figure is on display in the National Museum in Dublin.

Return to the R293 and turn right as far as the Edmondstown crossroads - 2.9 miles (4.66 km) from Carrowntemple - and turn left for Monasteraden. After one mile park your car at Lough Gara Cultural Resource Office at Clogher Hall, on the left (Tel. 0907 61067). Information on the area can be obtained here.

6 Clogher Cashel

Almost opposite here is the entrance to Clogher Cashel. Enter the gate and turn right following the wall for 20m. It is located on a rounded ridge and surrounded by mature woodland within Coolavin Demesne of the McDermott family. Most cashels belong to the Early Christian period (440-1200 AD), but some excavated examples have dated to earlier periods. Enclosed by a massive stone wall it is 26m in diameter and the walls are 4.3m thick and 2m high.. There are a number of souterrains present. These are underground structures, normally consisting of one or more passages and chambers. Usually they are drystone constructions but some are rock-cut. They functioned as places of refuge and storage and are common to many ringforts. The souterrains are dangerous and should not be entered.

A little further on the road towards Monasteraden, a short walk from the Cultural Resource Office is St Attracta's Well, which is just off the road to the left.

7 St Attracta's Well

The veneration of wells is a widespread and very ancient tradition in Ireland. The country was not swiftly converted to

Clogher Cashel

St Attracta's Well

Christianity and many pagan practises survived. Gradually, some aspects of paganism, such as sacred trees and wells, were incorporated into a Christian context. The deities worshipped at sacred wells or trees were generally replaced by a local patron saint of the early Irish church.

St Attracta's well has eight praying stones on top of the wall above the well. By turning these while praying pilgrims would hope to receive a blessing. Also at the well is a 17th century crucifixion plaque, known as a 'Penal Cross'. The well is said to have a cure for warts and possibly rickets. The cure is obtained from the water in the hollow of a large boulder at the foot of the well.

St Attracta was an important local saint who was baptised by St Patrick. There is the legend concerning St Attracta where it is said that she built her Nunnery where seven roads met, so that she might have a wide field in which to exercise hospitality.

Walk

A short walk from the well can be undertaken. Keep going up the narrow road that the well is on. This small road winds uphill. Turn back at the Y-junction if all you want is a stroll (15 minutes round trip) or fork left for a walk of approximately 1 hour. The road curves across a bog and

Sunset on Lough Gara

Lough Gara

some forestry with great views in all directions beginning to open up. It climbs to a T-junction and turn right to the top of a hill, where there is a glorious view over Lough Gara. Continue going to the next right which will bring you back to the Holy Well.

8 Lough Gara & Crannógs

Lough Gara has an important colony of Whooper Swans and White-breasted Geese among other bird colonies breeding on it. The lake is also well known for its crannógs. Crannógs are artificial islands which can be seen on the majority of Sligo's lakes. However, the greatest concentration of these is found here on Lough Gara when more than three hundred crannóg-type sites were revealed after a drainage scheme in 1952. Many appear as mounds in lakeshore marshy areas or as small islands. The name is derived from the Irish word *'crann'*, meaning a tree, which is a reference to the

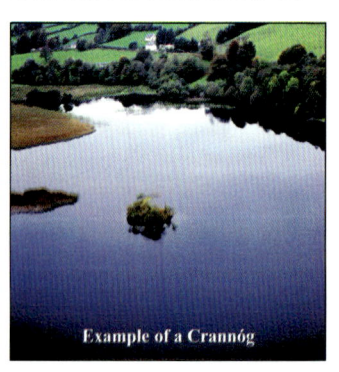

Example of a Crannóg

common usage of timber in their construction. Research has discovered that in prehistoric times platforms were erected at lake-edges or in shallow water or marshy ground and were principally associated with hunting, fishing or with industrial type pursuits, rather than with long-term habitation. However, a true crannóg is an artificial island containing a dwelling and surrounded by a palisade and these were constructed in the Early Christian

Whooper Swan

period, contemporary with ringforts.

More information can be obtained from the Moygara Cultural Resource Office at Clogher Hall.

Continue into the village of Monasteraden - a distance on 0.6 miles from St Attracta's Well. Go straight across at the crossroads but take the left fork down a narrow road. After 2.6 miles (4.2 km) you come to a hand ball alley. There is space to park your car here on the verge. Walk straight on from here and turn right, cross the fence carefully to visit Moygara Castle.

9 Moygara Castle

The castle of Moygara was the principle fortress and dwelling of the O'Gara family. In 1581 a body of Scottish mercenaries in the service of Captain Malby, Governor of Connacht, burned the building and killed many of the O'Garas. The building became disused apart from a brief period during the Williamite wars. The name O'Gara is one of the oldest in North Connacht. The castle stands on a slight eminence with great views, particularly to the south. The building consists of a plain rectangular tower set within a square bawn with flanking angled towers at each corner. All the gun loops in the castle are intact. On the ground at the western entrance there are two carved keystones, originally thought to have been Sheila na Gigs or exhibitionist figures. However, the first stone appears to be two figures sitting with their legs intertwined and the other is of a figure possibly holding an infant in its right hand.

Continue along the narrow road for a short distance heading straight from the hand ball alley to a T-junction where you turn right on to the R294 for Boyle. After 2.3 miles (3.7 km), and just before the village sign for Cloonloo, turn left at this crossroads along a narrow road. After the road bends to the left turn right under a railway bridge. Turn right again and the road gets even narrower. It begins to climb and reaches another T-junction after 1.7 miles (2.7 km). Turn left and 200m on your right is a lay-by.

10 Viewing Point

This attractive spot has a stone information plaque indicating what you can see across

Moygara Castle

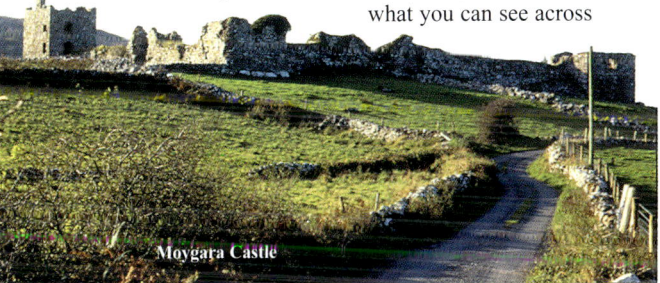

The southern side of the Bricklieve Mountains

the breath-taking views from here. as well as aspects of the areas history.

Turn your car and pass the road you came up, continuing straight on. You reach another T-junction after 0.5 miles (0.8 km), where you turn right. After 2.5 miles (4 km) you reach the R295 Boyle to Ballymote road and turn left towards Ballymote.

There are excellent views of the west side of the Bricklieve mountains as you drive along this road. After 6.7 miles (10.8 km) you reach a lay-by on the right hand side of the road. Park here to view Toomour Church.

11 Toomour

Next to the church is an early-Christian altar with praying stones and a cross slab with an unusual design carved on it. Archdeacon O'Rorke, who wrote "The History of Sligo Town and County" in the end of the last century claims that this *leacht*, or altar was in fact a "Royal Mausoleum" built as the grave to Irish kings who fell in battle after the battle of Ceis Corainn, fought nearby in 971 AD, between the Northerners and the men of Connacht. The *leacht* and stones date possibly to the 6th century AD, but there could have been internments there during the 10th century.

O'Rorke also ties this in with a nearby well called Kings-town Well, saying it got is name from the dead king buried near the church. However, folklore says otherwise. Kings-town Well is a mis-pronounciation of King-stone Well, which in turn seems to be a mis-translation. *Cloich Righ* means 'Kings-stone' but a similar sounding *Cluiche Righ* means 'Game of Kings', the medieval name given to the Black Death and there is a legend associated with the well that it was used as a holy cure for the plague.

Archdeacon O'Rorke also claims that the famous hermit of Glendalough in County Wicklow - St Kevin - came to Toomour to be ordained by its Bishop

Toomour Church

Leacht at Toomour

Lughigh around the year 560 AD and that the place became an important place of pilgrimage. The present Roman Catholic church is called St Kevin's

You reach Keash Village after a further 1.3 miles (2.9 km). Park at the Post office, after passing the small shop and petrol station. The Post Office has a tourist information point and coffee shop.

12 Keshcorran

On the summit of Keshcorran Mountain (362m) stands the 'Pinnacle', a large unopened cairn surrounded by a large oval shaped enclosure 80m across, which is visible for many miles.

On the west face of the mountain are 17 caves located near Keash Village. Some of these were explored in 1901 and again in 1929. Bones of reindeer, deer, boar, wolf and arctic lemmings were found along with a large variety of birds including rare or extinct species. Bears and foxes seemed

Kestral and his lunch!

to have occupied the caves for long periods, rearing their young and dragging in deer, portions of horses, hares, pigs, field mice and frogs. Early man seems to have occasionally visited the caves, perhaps while on hunting expeditions, as charcoal deposits were found. However, his presence was not frequent, perhaps because of the bears. From the 8th to the 11th centuries there were more signs of human presence in the caves remains of fires, domestic and wild animal bones, shellfish debris, and various implements and articles of personal adornment were found.

The Lughnasa festival in honour of the Celtic god Lugh was held in front of the caves on Garland Sunday, the last Sunday in July. In olden times the festival lasted three days and local tribes came together. In modern times the local sports day is held on this Sunday with dancing in the evening. Many people still make their way to the caves.

The caves have a huge number of associated legends, one of which relates the birth of Cormac McAirt. Cormac's father was High King of Ireland who was slain by the usurper Lughaidh McCon. While the late King's wife was fleeing from Tara to friends in Connacht, she gave birth

Cormac's Cave

to Cormac near Keash. As mother and baby were sleeping on a bed of leaves, the child was reputedly stolen by a she-wolf. A few years later Cormac was discovered outside the Caves of Keash playing on all fours with his foster brothers, the wolf cubs. Cormac later became a famous High King of Ireland.

Many stories relate adventures concerning Fionn MacCumhaill and the Fianna as they frequented this area for its excellent hunting. One of the tales is called *Bruidean Cheise* which tells how Fionn, while sitting on the cairn on the summit of the mountain, watching his Fianna hunting on the plains of Corran, is lured and trapped by three hideous hags. They manage to capture the entire Fianna in the cairn and bind them with cords woven by enchantment. The description of the hags show what Fionn and his men were up against!

"Their hair was black as ink and tough as wire; it stuck up and poked out and hung down about their heads in bushes and spikes and tangles. Their eyes were bleary and red. Their mouths were black and twisted, and in each of these mouths there was a hedge of curved yellow fangs ... they had moustaches poking under their noses and woolly wads growing out of their ears, so that when you looked at them the first time you never wanted to look at them again, and if you looked at them a second time you were likely to die of the sight." Fortunately for Fionn and the Fianna they were rescued at the last minute by Goll MacMorna who fought in fierce combat with the hags and killed them all.

It was also in this area that Diarmait and Gráinne settled after their flight from Fionn (see pg. 33).

Walks

A short walk from the Post Office heading back down towards Boyle can be undertaken (45 minutes).

Turn off the R295 towards St Kevin's RC Church. Turn left at the T-junction (the church is to the right) Continue along the narrow lane and pass the left turning. The caves are now above you on the right. Return to the turn (now on your right) and go down it, turning left at end to rejoin your car. Alternatively walk from Post Office towards Ballymote turn right and turn left to get to the caves. The landowner is Mr John Freehill. Access to the caves is very steep and the caves can be very unsafe to enter; extreme care should be exercised if visiting them.

Return to Ballymote - 4.5 miles (7.24 km) from here - to complete the tour.